Discovering Humor in the Bible

Discovering Humor in the Bible

AN EXPLORER'S GUIDE

Howard R. Macy

CASCADE *Books* · Eugene, Oregon

DISCOVERING HUMOR IN THE BIBLE
An Explorer's Guide

Copyright © 2016 Howard R. Macy. All rights reserved. Except for brief quotations in critical publications or reviews, no part of this book may be reproduced in any manner without prior written permission from the publisher. Write: Permissions, Wipf and Stock Publishers, 199 W. 8th Ave., Suite 3, Eugene, OR 97401.

Cascade Books
An Imprint of Wipf and Stock Publishers
199 W. 8th Ave., Suite 3
Eugene, OR 97401

www.wipfandstock.com

PAPERBACK ISBN: 978-1-4982-9259-7
HARDCOVER ISBN: 978-1-4982-9261-0
EBOOK ISBN: 978-1-4982-9260-3

Cataloguing-in-Publication data:

Names: Macy, Howard R.

Title: Discovering humor in the Bible : an explorer's guide / Howard R. Macy.

Description: Eugene, OR: Cascade Books, 2016 | Includes bibliographical references.

Identifiers: ISBN 978-1-4982-9259-7 (paperback) | ISBN 978-1-4982-9261-0 (hardcover) | ISBN 978-1-4982-9260-3 (ebook)

Subjects: LCSH: Wit and humor in the Bible | Wit and humor—Theology

Classification: BS680.W63 M12 2016 (print) | BS680.W63 M12 (ebook)

Manufactured in the U.S.A. JULY 13, 2016

Scripture taken from the Common English Bible®, CEB® Copyright © 2010, 2011 by Common English Bible.™ Used by permission. All rights reserved worldwide. The "CEB" and "Common English Bible" trademarks are registered in the United States Patent and Trademark Office by Common English Bible. Use of either trademark requires the permission of Common English Bible.

Scripture quotations from THE MESSAGE. Copyright © by Eugene H. Peterson 1993, 1994, 1995, 1996, 2000, 2001, 2002. Used by permission of NavPress. All rights reserved. Represented by Tyndale House Publishers, Inc.

For
Derric, Asher, and Katelyn
with love and gladness

Contents

Acknowledgments ix
Abbreviations x
Introduction: An Invitation xi

I. DISCOVERING HUMOR

1. Why Humor in the Bible? 3
2. How Do You Read? 10
3. What Do You Look For? 16
4. What If You Find It? 25

II. FIELD GUIDES FOR EXPLORERS

The Founding Family 33
Humor in the Stories about Joseph 38
Humor in Judges 39
Humor about David: Hero on the Run 43
Humor in the Early Prophets 46
Humor in the Story about Esther 49
Humor in the Wisdom Literature 51
Humor in the Prophetic Books 54
Humor in the Apocrypha 58
Introduction to Jesus' Use of Humor 60
Jesus' Funny Encounters 61
Jesus' Funny Characters 63
Jesus' Funny Images 66
Jesus' Funny Miracles 68

Humor in the Gospel of John 71
Humor in Acts 74
Humor in Paul 77

III. REPORTS FROM THE FIELD

The Unhidden Revealed 83
God, That's Funny 85
Funny and Ugly 87
The *Voila!* Moment 90
Donkey-Speak 92
Mayhem, Shenanigans, and Hanky-Panky 95
David's Daring Dowry 97
Awful Funny 98
Covered with Glory 100
Witty Wisdom 102
Humor in Job? 104
Women of Valor 106
The Hilarity of Grace 108
Hubbub and Incarnation 110
Stand-Up Jesus 113
Imagine Them Smiling 115
Funnier than John 117
Try Head First 119
Easter Laughter 120
Smiling Persuasion 122

Select Bibliography 125

Acknowledgements

Hearty thanks to the many people who have encouraged and helped as this project has unfolded.

Thanks to my family for their patience and care. Readers can thank especially Margi Macy and Nate Macy, whose thoughtful reading has spared them some nonsense.

Thanks to my terrific colleagues at George Fox University for encouraging me, and especially to Paul Anderson, who opened the way for me to teach the course "Humor and the Bible."

Thanks to my students in that course, to both those who laughed and those who seemed perplexed. They all taught me a lot. Thanks also to the smart folks who engaged these ideas with me at Newberg Friends Church and Reedwood Friends Church.

Thanks to friends in our writers' group who cheered me on.

Thanks to editor Robin Parry and the other fine folk at Wipf & Stock for turning my high hopes into a book.

Abbreviations

CEB *Common English Bible*
KJV *King James Version*
LB *The Living Bible*
NJPS *The New JPS Translation*
NIV *New International Version*
NLT *New Living Translation*
TM *The Message*

Introduction: An Invitation

After a long journey, I'm writing to invite you to join me in discovering humor in the Bible, whether or where it is and what to make of it if you find it. You'll figure out soon enough what I think is funny, but that's not the point. Instead of telling harrowing tales of exploration and offering museum cases filled with captured prey, I want to create a field guide to help you explore on your own.

The idea of field guide comes from my trying to learn how to be a better bird-watcher. Whether it's a Sibley or a Peterson or *Bird Watching for Dummies*, such guides start by describing the tools you'll need, where to look, and what to look for. Of course, you first have to expect to see birds and actually look for them. (For some folks, that's already an advanced move.) Then it helps to have a good pair of binoculars. After that, you have to pay attention to all the ways birds differ from one another: body shapes, flight patterns, size, colors, beaks, length and color of legs, songs, where they hang out, how they move, and more. This field guide to exploring humor in the Bible helps in a similar way. It will talk about tools, habits, where to look, and what to look for. It won't say much about clothes to wear and bug spray.

This is a friendly invitation. For one thing, if you haven't seen humor in the Bible, I won't scold you or accuse you of being willfully stupid or humor-impaired. I haven't called this book *Bible Humor for Dummies* for two reasons. For one thing, I don't want to get sued. More importantly, though, I don't think my readers are stupid. Also, I won't coerce you. You can wander along, curious about what we're doing, without thinking you have to agree. In fact, you'll be free to write me an angry letter or post a review about how wrong and dangerous this book is, and I'll welcome that. Now if you think we're on to something here and want to say something nice, that would be fine, too. Any way you talk about it might help sales.

This project came about fairly respectably. This isn't one of those hidden-and-repressed-secrets-of-the-Bible-now-revealed sorts of books, though there's a good market for stuff like that. So I won't flirt with titles like *Is the Bible a Joke?* (I don't think). Instead, my exploring of humor in the Bible came out of teaching classes about biblical interpretation. One of the main principles for interpreting the Bible is that readers need to identify what sort of literature they're dealing with and then interpret the text accordingly. Lament songs, indictment speeches, parables, and various kinds of storytelling, for example, all need to be treated differently. This is a commonplace guide for people who want to take the Bible seriously and understand it rightly. What surprised me while teaching, though, was that handbooks about biblical interpretation scarcely mention humor. What happens if the Bible uses humor? What does it look like, why is it there, and what do you do with it if you find it?

Exploring such questions matters. You don't learn to recognize the Bible's humor simply as a side hobby or as an attempt to add light entertainment to Bible reading. You search it out because you want to know what the biblical writers actually meant to say. I assume that writers used humor on purpose in order to drive their message home. When we see the humor they intended, it often clarifies and sharpens their point. If we don't see it, we can miss their point badly, sometimes with disastrous results.

So I made interpreting humor in the Bible a project. Maybe I could do something useful, even get a respectable scholarly paper out of it. (Actually, sometimes people, including me, do present serious papers about humor.) I was already convinced that the Bible used humor. Some texts, like all the laughter about Abraham and Sarah having a baby in their old age, use it so obviously that you can hardly say otherwise. And I had already read authors who discuss humor in the Bible, at that point most notably Elton

Trueblood's *The Humor of Christ*. I continued to read widely and to experiment, altogether a fun and interesting adventure.

Knowing of my interest, Paul Anderson, my friend and at that time my department chair, wondered whether I would like to teach a class on humor and the Bible. Absolutely! Eventually I got to offer it several times, and students taught me a lot. They came into the class not knowing what to think. Some were simply curious. Others were relieved, since they had laughed privately at stuff in the Bible but were afraid to say so. Others were openly skeptical, but only occasionally violent and hostile. We had lots of fun learning and laughing through the course. But what they said when they had finished the class caught me off guard. Of course, they had learned a lot about humor and how various interpreters saw it in Scripture. More than that, though, they often reported that the Bible had become more accessible to them and that they were more eager to read it. One student who knew the Bible very well wrote that, with these insights, it was "like reading the Bible for the first time." Others responded that through our study they had come to richer understandings of God and Jesus, ones that opened up new dimensions in their lives.

So through my own exploration and through my teaching about humor in the Bible, I've become convinced that it's important to help people experiment with this. For many, perhaps for you, it may help them become better Bible readers and it may open new paths in their life with God. That's why I'm writing and why I'm inviting you to join me in this adventure in Bible reading.

I.

Discovering Humor

1.

Why Humor in the Bible?

WHY WOULD THE BIBLE use humor? Why would you look for it there? After all, the Bible is a serious book; people look to it to guide their lives. It shows us how to relate to God and to each other. It's supposed to tell the truth, not crack jokes.

Asking such questions is partly right, given some of the ways that we use humor in our culture. Many folks see humor as merely flippant or frivolous and they dismiss it as light entertainment. So it's easy to forget that funny isn't always just for fun. Also, people often use humor to belittle or to poke fun, and Bible readers sure don't want to ridicule or discredit Scripture. Frankly, because so much of contemporary humor relies on insults and the rude and crude, it's no surprise that some folks are jumpy about associating humor with the Bible.

Actually, humor at its best is a gift. It offers a gracious reality check to help us reflect on, or just get glimpses of, our powers, our limits, and our frailty. We need laughter when we discover, once again, that our best plans turn out to be losers. Or when catastrophes erupt when we have everything under control. Without humor we can get grim and get trapped in denial. With humor we can step back, look from another angle, and imagine new possibilities. A lot of the Bible's humor celebrates—surprise! surprise!— that there is power and possibility that transcends our frailty.

But wait, there's more! Humor can work wonders. Not only can it relieve stress, make you healthier, and help relationships run smoothly, it can tell the truth and make you smile. Oscar Wilde once called attention to humor as a health benefit: "If you want to tell people the truth, make them laugh, otherwise they'll kill you." Apart from not getting killed, however, I'm going to skip the health benefits here (you've probably seen tons of articles about that) and go directly to saying it's fine if the Bible sometimes entertains you and even makes you laugh out loud.

A young man once told me how the Bible unexpectedly made him laugh out loud. He had become a Christian during his college years and decided that now he needed to read the Bible. So he started at the beginning, read lots of stories, ploughed through instructions about how to gather manna and offer animal sacrifice, through battles won and lost, and even more until he came to the story of David faking insanity by rolling on the ground and foaming at the mouth when the guards at an enemy town identified him (wrongly) as "the King of Israel." The guards then took him to their King Achish, who said, "Can't you see he's crazy? Why bring him to me? Am I short on insane people that you've brought this person to go crazy right in front of me? Do you really think I'm going to let this man enter my house?" (1 Samuel 21:14–15 CEB). Suddenly, my friend laughed out loud! Here's a priceless, throw-away laugh line. How could you not laugh? And how could the writer not include a line like "Am I short on insane people . . . ?" even if it's not to make a theological point? I was glad my friend laughed, even though he had missed a lot more funny stuff on the way. (It's funny, too, that crazy David later went to work for this king. And hoodwinked him. So the laugh also points to David's shrewdness and the king's gullibility.)

Humor engages us. It can capture us, pique our interest, and keep us involved. We like teachers and storytellers who have a sense of humor, who can draw us along with a funny word picture or turn of phrase. Sometimes they use humor to make our favorite characters even more endearing. For example, Abraham falls on the ground laughing (ROFL), not in awe, right in front of God when God tells him that at 100 years old he'll be a father. Young David's brothers trash-talk him when he brashly asks

Israel's soldiers why Goliath scares everyone. Funny stories of near escapes and mischievous exploits often add charm to our heroes.

Humor helps us remember, too. Laughter makes our brains stickier. That's one reason that short sayings like proverbs often include funny images or word-play. I often remember the wise and funny advice, "If you wake your friend early in the morning by shouting 'Rise and shine!,' it will sound to him more like a curse than a blessing" (Proverbs 27:14, *The Message*). And who can forget stories about a short guy who scrambles up a tree to see Jesus or about the daring disciple who starts to walk on water then sinks like a rock?

Humor can also sneak up on you and whack you on the side of the head. Or slip in the back door of your thinking while you're fiercely guarding the front. Or scramble your well-ordered ideas and leave you thinking, "Say what?!" Jesus often did that with parables. I suspect that Jesus' disciples both smiled and scratched their heads wondering what in the world he meant by telling the story about a rich man who commended his dishonest manager for being clever (Luke 16).

Best of all, humor doesn't just crack jokes, it tells the truth. Sometimes it's the very best way, maybe the only way, to tell the truth. In the Bible that's partly because God acts in such absurd and outlandish ways. "A good joke," writes Frederick Buechner, "is one that catches you by surprise—like God's, for instance. Who would have guessed that Israel of all nations would be the one God picked or Sarah would have Isaac at the age of ninety or the Messiah would turn up in a manger? . . . The laugh in each case results from astonished delight at the sheer unexpectedness of the thing. . . . When God really gets going, even the morning stars burst into singing and all the sons of God shout for joy" (*Beyond Words*, 162–63).

The Bible revels in its menagerie of unlikely heroes, of folks who said, "Who me? Do what!?" Its Hall of Fame shows off winners that made people say, "Who woulda thunk that he (or she!) would rescue us?!" It gives us tale after tale of comic reversals and narrow escapes. It tells stories of messy relationships, often awkward and funny. And as the Bible speaks of grace, that gift itself dazzles with absurdity and surprise. If we're smart, we welcome it. How can we not laugh, too, and sing and shout for joy?

Comedy writers know that humor often grows out of tragedy plus time. Humor gives us perspective. Harrowing tales can become humorous stories without undercutting the tragedy and terror of the first moments. For example, 1 Samuel contains many episodes about the decline of Saul and the steady peril of David, who is betrayed and running for his life. The narrators keep the tragic core, but they also can make us laugh by showing the bigger-than-life absurdities in the stories and portraying David sometimes as an uncanny escape artist and trickster.

Think, too, of Belshazzar throwing a huge festival to celebrate his being invincible, the king of the cosmos. The storytellers had to be going for a laugh when they tell us that when Belshazzar saw a hand writing on the wall, "his limbs gave way ["the joints of his loins were loosened" (JPS)] and his knees knocked together." The laugh takes nothing away from the terrifying moment. For Israel's storytellers, humor heightens it and deepens the celebration of God's liberating act.

I find both high-stake drama and humor in the story about Paul and Barnabas visiting the city of Lystra. After they healed a man crippled from birth, the astonished locals decided that Paul and Barnabas were the gods Zeus and Hermes, and they brought bulls and wreaths to make sacrifices to them. The missionaries barely kept them from it, all the while protesting, "People, what are you doing? We are humans too, just like you!" and speaking to them about God's goodness. In a sudden turn, the crowd quit trying to sacrifice, stoned Paul instead, and left him for dead. He later got back up and walked to town—and left the next day. At one level this is a tragic story, filled with confusion and violence. At another, though, the joyful healing, the crowd's lavish surge to worship, and the abrupt reversal toward stoning all share over-the-top surprises that can make us giggle.

Even though the Bible uses humor generously and for good reasons, a lot of folks miss it or even don't want to see it. Of course, some folks may not have a sense of humor, but nobody will admit that, so we're not going there. Yet some people with a great sense of humor can't imagine that the Bible, serious as it is, would include humor, so they don't expect it and don't look for it. That's more innocent than actively resisting the idea because what you believe about how the Bible has to work leaves humor out completely. If you've read this far, that probably doesn't include you.

Many readers simply don't know what to look for. If we think that humor in the Bible mostly looks like stand-up comedy or telling jokes, we won't see much of that. Nor will we discover humorous writing in the styles of Mark Twain, Dave Barry, Patrick McManus, or Erma Bombeck. But humor has many devices and forms, which we'll introduce shortly in this field guide. We'll also suggest ways of reading that can help us see what's there.

Sometimes people will miss the Bible's humor because they know the Bible so well. It's too familiar. They already "know" what's there, so may read inattentively, a bit hurried and numb. Or they may read too intensely, trying to wring every drop of meaning out of the text. When people I'm with are convulsively serious, I love throwing in a non sequitur or a bit of silliness and watching it fly by completely unnoticed. Or seeing a delayed smile or brain sproing. This can happen in Bible reading, too. Readers who know the Bible well can learn to read with new eyes.

Other folks don't know the Bible quite well enough. They may not know the longer storylines that provide context and background detail for individual stories. To see the humor in the sister fights between Leah and Rachel, for instance, it helps to know the backstory of how they both became Jacob's wives and of how one became a baby factory while the other was barren. Similarly, knowing what a fighting family Joseph's brothers were helps set up his quip when he sends them from Egypt to bring his father, "Don't quarrel along the way." Some readers may not have absorbed enough of cultures foreign to us to catch the glaring mistakes and awkwardness that both create and signal humor. For example, you have to understand how devoted a kosher kid Peter was when he had a vision in which he was offered, and told to eat, distinctly non-kosher foods—ham sandwiches, cheeseburgers, lobster, and more—a whole buffet full. Once you see how startling and outrageous it is, you can also see its humor. For that matter, it helps to know what kosher dietary laws meant to Jewish folk in his time. The good news is that readers who don't know the Bible well can both expand their knowledge and sharpen their eyes.

Found humor versus created humor

Please remember that my goal here is not to introduce humor into the Bible or to joke about the Bible, but to discover where biblical writers have intentionally used humor. To honor that difference, I find it useful to distinguish between "created humor" and "found humor." Created humor is when we play with the text in ways that make us laugh. Found humor is when we see how an author has used humor to make us laugh. Both are fine, in my judgment, but we need to honor the difference.

Probably most of us have used "created humor" in reading the Bible. Many of us have told jokes or asked questions about Noah, for example: What did he do with the termites? Who had to shovel out the bottom of the boat? What kind of crazy things did his neighbors say to him? Or we might have joked about eating manna for forty years and wondered about manna recipes—manna burgers, mannacotti, bamanna bread, etc. You may have wondered with me whether Abraham's entourage objected when they learned the sign of the covenant was to be circumcision: "Say what?! Couldn't we just shake hands?" Or maybe we've chuckled about Lazarus stumbling out of his tomb in grave clothes, smelling bad, and startled to see such a crowd. In some instances we may play with or elaborate a bit on the humor the writers have given us, a kind of middle ground, but we do need to know when we, not the author, have brought the humor.

Sometimes readers will laugh at names or practices that seem odd to them, but that mostly comes from the huge cultural distance between our time and theirs. When we were expecting our first child, I teased my mother that we would name him

Maher-shalal-hash-baz, what Isaiah named one of his sons. I laughed; she was somewhere between amused and terrified. I'm not sure Isaiah's kid ever laughed about it. Sometimes writers use names and name-changes in funny ways. For example, the Hebrew name Nabal means "fool" (some study Bible footnotes will tell you that), and the story about him in 1 Samuel 25 plays that to the hilt. But often when we laugh at names, we're introducing created humor.

So also with cultural practices that seem odd to us. One that even the Bible needed to explain was how a guy took off his sandal and handed it to Boaz to seal a deal that let Boaz buy a field and take Ruth as his wife. I know a lot of folks have laughed at the prospect that we might take off our shoes to make a deal. We might rightly expect to find many ancient practices that make us giggle a bit.

By distinguishing between created and found humor we can learn to see where the biblical writers have intended to use humor and try to understand what they were up to.

2.

How Do You Read?

To see humor in the Bible, most of us need to change how we normally read. In the rush of our lives, many of us read quickly, skim, or even "retinize" the text, letting the image of the page bounce off the back of our eyeballs. We'll breeze through the news, snag a weird or snarky headline, glance at sports scores or stock prices, and quickly check the obits to see if we're still alive. Maybe on a slow day we'll catch a cartoon. We tend to control the text, grab what we want, and ignore the rest. We do this routinely with newspapers, social media, magazines, manuals, textbooks, mail, and much more. It's frankly utilitarian and unimaginative, and though we lose a lot in the process, fast reading is often quite practical.

This is rarely, however, a practical or fruitful way to read the Bible. Instead of cherry-picking, managing, and working on the text, we need to let the text work on us. We need to read the Bible in ways that let it shape us, teach us, surprise us, catch us off guard, and give us new eyes. That requires different approaches to reading.

One obvious step is simply to slow down, relax a bit, and let the text breathe. Be open to surprise, serendipity, and the "aha" of discovery. It's not the style of tourists in a hurry, running by magnificent sites while checking off of their to-do lists the what, when, where, and how much of their travel. ("This is Tuesday; it must be Paris. This is Friday; it must be Zechariah.") Instead, it's more standing still, eyes wide open, trying to take in all that's there, seeing shapes and details, colors and textures, grandeur and movement, and then looking even more. Enter expectantly and with your senses on full alert. You might see an eagle soar, or hear a warbler sing, or spot a chameleon scurrying by. We'll explore that more shortly.

Let the text decompress. Frankly, the biblical text is often quite compact and may not include details that normally would create a whole scene. In Mark 6, for example, a storm comes up on the Sea of Galilee, Jesus walks on water, joins the disciples, and calms the storm, all in less than 100 words. In Acts 17, Paul and Silas stir up an uproar in Thessalonica in just eight Bible verses. Or, put another way, using a moderate pace, you can read out loud Jesus' story about the unforgiving servant, one of his longer stories, in less than two minutes. The story about catching a fish with a coin in his mouth to pay the temple tax takes less than a minute. The whole Sermon on the Mount read aloud takes maybe fifteen. My hunch is that it took Jesus or the early apostles longer than that.

Many action stories are told in 100–200 words. They give interesting detail, but leave a lot unsaid. Others are longer, but still leave gaps that invite readers to enter the story. Sometimes entering a text also includes taking the long view, relating details and clues we know from outside a particular text to help create a whole picture. For example, we have a series of stories about Abraham and his heirs or stories about shepherd-to-king David, and this larger network of stories often provides background and clues that help readers understand any single narrative.

Of course, written texts often leave out clues that would normally create the whole scene. We don't get hints of pause or pace, tone of voice, facial expression, gesture, and certainly not laugh tracks or cue cards (though I suppose, without my urging, that entrepreneurial digital Bible publishers could add laugh tracks). So readers have to actively enter the texts to hear and see, to smell and touch and taste. We have to use our senses and our imagination. Actually, in doing this we are not using our imaginations alone; we are not just making stuff up. We are, instead, letting the words do their work. Words describe actions and objects, they point to a scene and invite us to see it. So part of our reading is to try to see what they picture.

To let the scenes come alive for us, we can actively use our senses. What did it look like, for instance, to see ninety-year-old Sarah shuffling along in geriatric maternity clothes, laughing when people laughed and promising that everyone would laugh? What kind of public display of affection did Isaac shower on his "sister" (wife) Rebekah that made the folks in Gerar say, "Hey, that's not his 'sister'!"? Can we see and hear enough of Sinai's rock-shattering rumble and lightning storms to feel some of the Hebrews' fear on the plain below? My friend Canby's eyes would flash and his voice giggle when he read aloud from Psalm 114 and saw its images, "Why is it, O sea, that you flee?/ O Jordan, that you turn back?/ O mountains that you skip like rams?/ O hills, like lambs?" He let the visual live.

One wonders what it would sound like to hear brash, too-young, lunch-carrier David yell out to the Israelite troops quivering in front of Goliath, "What's everyone so scared of?" Maybe we could hear the scold in his soldier brothers' put-down response. Or maybe while David is playing music to soothe Saul, we could hear the sound of the harp interrupted by the thunk of Saul's spear piercing the wall. Perhaps we can enter into conversations, trying to hear the tone of voice, to notice pauses, and to wonder whether faces might show smiles, frowns, or puzzlement.

What would it be like to savor the text when it speaks of Torah or Lady Wisdom's words as being "sweeter than honey"? What would it feel like to reach through a crowd to touch the hem of Jesus' cloak? Or to feel Jesus touch your eyes so that, for the first time, you can see? What might it smell like to enter a great banquet hall or to catch a whiff of the rot of war? What would it feel like to strain to draw in a net about to burst with an outsized catch of fish?

Some readers find it helpful to enter the scene. Perhaps you could try simply being a bystander, trying to take in what's happening. Or you might become one of the characters to understand what they experience. Or you might interview the players in the story to see what they might tell you. These time-tested methods often bring new insight.

It helps me sometimes, as a word-and-text person, to jump-start my thinking by perusing visual images that prompt my seeing. The striking illuminations in *The St. John's Bible*, for example, open new, unexpected vistas. "Coffee table books" that picture scenes from ancient and modern Israel can help create a reservoir of images that deepen understanding and clarity. Photographs and artists' work of illustration or imaginative reconstruction advance our ability to see. In a similar way, we can probably experiment with sharpening our senses of taste, touch, smelling, and hearing.

These examples suggest how we can use our senses and imagination, not to read into the text, but to let the text spring to life and draw us in. Though I see this as a path to discovering humor in the Bible, this approach to reading can help all of our Bible reading flourish.

Another approach that often helps is to read the Bible aloud. Let me reveal a pet peeve here. I don't mean read aloud with the flat, fast, boring robotic voice that you often hear when people read the Bible. (To put it ever so gently, that desecrates Scripture.) I mean reading aloud in a way that hearers can picture what the text describes and can grasp, without following a written text, what it's trying to say. Of course, in exploring a story or a teaching, you can do this just for yourself as both reader and hearer. It's a wonderful way to learn.

Reading aloud, whether poorly or well, interprets the Bible. To do it well, you have to wrestle with what the text is trying to picture and what it means to say. Then you have to experiment with how to read to convey those meanings. Folks who study oral interpretation learn to ask, "What's being pictured here? What are the key words? Which words belong together and how do they flow? How fast or slow does it need to go? Where do pauses belong? What should the voice sound like—questioning, boasting, angry, skeptical, confessing, puzzled, playful, teasing, banter?" These questions are all experiments in interpretation, and they help us understand the text.

Be the storyteller. Like a lot of folks, I love to read aloud to my kids and grandkids; before we had kids, my wife and I enjoyed reading aloud to each other. (After a stressful week, a favorite for fun and wipe-your-eyes laughter were stories of Winnie the Pooh.) I've loved it even more when the grandkids learned to read aloud to me and to read with expression, trying to show what was going on in the story. We can read the Bible that way, too.

A warning: sometimes people read the Bible too slowly, or maybe better, in a way that disconnects the flow of the text. I've seen folks try so hard to squeeze deep meaning out of every verse that they miss the funny lines. Sometimes they'll miss humor that strengthens the point. Other times they may try to get deep meaning out of a funny, throw-away line. For example, when guards bring crazy-acting David to King Achish, he says, "Why are you bringing this crazy man into my court? Don't I have enough crazy people here already?" It's great for a laugh, but probably not the basis for a three-point sermon. Of course, I could be wrong.

All in all, I invite you to explore ways of reading the Bible. Be willing to hold things loosely, to experiment, to ask "what if?"—even to be playful—as you listen deeply to the text.

Choosing helpful translations

Read from Bibles that sound normal to you. Their language should sound and feel like what you hear and use every day. Probably not exactly like all the language you hear, of course. But language from the "real world," not like "Biblish" (a term borrowed from Gordon Fee and Mark Strauss) that tells you right off that you've entered an ethereal dimension removed from your ordinary life. For a variety of reasons, some folks like Biblish, but its unnatural feel hinders discovering humor. The first readers and hearers of biblical texts found them natural and ordinary. So should we.

Let's just tiptoe on the edges of the flap about Bible translation. All good translators want to create a text that will accurately convey the Bible's meaning. Those who insist on translating word-for-word usually offer a text that feels a bit stiff or stilted. Those who work more from meaning-to-meaning usually offer translations that seem more fluent or natural. For our purposes, the second type of translation will help us more. We'll catch humor more easily in normal language.

The more fluent group offers several options. The title of one of the newest translations, The *Common English Bible* (CEB), describes its goal, wanting to use ordinary language that will also make sense when read aloud. The *New Living Translation* (NLT) descends from the popular paraphrase, the *Living Bible* (LB). Eugene Peterson's paraphrase, *The Message* (TM), has gathered many readers since its language is so accessible to modern readers. Another newer translation, *The Voice*, tries to reach readers who are new to Bible reading and shapes the text for that purpose. Another paraphrase, using more liberty than most, but still responsibly conveying meaning, is Clarence Jordan's *Cotton Patch* versions of the Gospels and other New Testament texts. You may find still others. Over the years I have also enjoyed the *Jerusalem Bible*, N. T. Wright's *The Kingdom New Testament*, and others. You may know others that work well for you. If you're fluent in Elizabethan English and easily get all of Shakespeare's jokes, you might enjoy the *King James Version* (KJV) or its sound-alikes (KJVXXIII and the like).

You may want to experiment with several versions rather than settling down to one, even if you eventually lean toward one or two of them as favorites. Reading in several can yield a richer, more nuanced sense of what the text is doing.

3.

What Do You Look For?

A FIELD GUIDE ABOUT birds, wildflowers, geology, or animal scat gives users cues about what to look for. With birds, for example, it will describe shape, size, coloring, sound, habitat, and behavior, often in exquisite detail. It helps users to know where to look and how to look. What I want to share here are cues for recognizing humor in the Bible. It's not so much to explain the joke or tell you what I think is funny, though that will show. Instead, I want to help you stay open to humor and find ways to wonder, "Could that be funny?"

Of course, people's senses of humor vary a lot. Some folks seem to see funny easily, often, and all over the place. They might even annoy you, though I love hanging out with people who see funny. We may laugh more quickly at some humor devices than others, whether puns, absurdity, or exaggeration. In our explorations here, it helps to know that we're wired differently and that we can disagree.

I suspect that different wirings are part of God's gift to our communities. Some see funny, some quickly empathize, others go quickly to the heart of a message. We're a glorious mix, which is why we need to read together, respect each other, and depend on one another. Also, we all bring different experiences. I've learned especially to try to listen to the wisdom of women who know stuff that an ordinary man just doesn't get. In looking for the Bible's humor, I remember seeing women nodding and laughing in unison over things I had just breezed by, such as the sister spats between Leah and Rachel. Cherishing our varied gifts and experiences sharpens our vision.

Cultures also use humor differently or value some forms over others. A friend who lived in Bolivia, for example, told me folks he knew there find trickster stories and jokes hilarious. The biblical storytellers themselves clearly love exaggeration as one of their comic tools. Though we see differences and favorites, however, the common devices of humor play well across cultures.

When we read the Bible, it helps to remember that we are engaging with cultures quite foreign to our own. With humor, it helps me to try to see things through their eyes and to wonder why the first audience, the Israelites, would laugh. Frankly, sometimes they'll use humor in ways I don't like, but I still can see why they would laugh and how it would have served them. I can see, for example, why they might laugh at the downfall of their oppressors, or make fun of enemies as fat and stupid, or roar with delight over tricks Israelites played on their foes.

Despite individual and cultural differences, some basic humor devices work nearly everywhere. We'll look first at three common forms, noting that they often overlap, and then we'll explore some variations and sometimes puzzling uses of humor.

A detour on keeping it simple. You don't have to learn Hebrew and Greek to do this. Sure, the Bible includes humor that depends on word-play in its original languages and that doesn't work in whatever language you speak. If you could easily carry on a conversation in ancient Hebrew and Greek, you might get the joke. Of course, you'd have to be pretty good at it. I know folks who don't get word play in their native language. So let's learn the humor of word-play from people who know the biblical languages. The rest of these devices apply in whatever language works for you.

Surprise. Surprise prompts people to laugh by suddenly giving them something they didn't expect or by abruptly changing direction. In physical comedy, a pratfall or an odd gesture or facial expression can get a laugh. Writers can use a surprising word or phrase to make a point and make you smile. (One of my favorites is

Ann Lamott's "Laughter is carbonated holiness.") Most jokes work by leading the hearer or reader one direction and closing with a punch-line that abruptly goes another. Unexpected outcomes and sudden reversals are at the heart of surprise. Trickster themes also bring surprise and laughter, whether we are being tricked or are enjoying the tricks of others.

Many biblical stories include surprise. The Gospels, for example, include a couple of stories about fishermen going suddenly from lousy fishing to a break-your-nets catch. Surprises and twists abound in the story of David and his soldiers who were hiding in a cave from Saul's army when suddenly Saul himself steps into their hiding place to relieve himself. Tricks and surprises carry the storyline of how Jacob related to his father-in-law Laban. Daniel's friends singing, not screaming, in a fiery furnace catches us off guard. And how about Jesus turning the water in large ritual purification jars into fine wine?

Funny-fit. If you want to say "humorous juxtaposition," that's fine with me. But this is a category where things just look funny together. It could be large and small, tall and short, fat and thin, smart and stupid, all categories of comedy that are well worn. It could be categories like irony or paradox. It could be what's odd, awkward, or absurd. It might be an unexpected hero like Gideon. He's hiding from the enemy, grinding grain in an olive press, when a messenger from God sneaks up and says, "Greetings, valiant warrior!" Gideon adds to the humor by explaining exactly why he is not and can't be a hero. Funny-fit might be mismatches in characters and actions, like Balaam the "seer," who doesn't know what's going on, and his donkey, who both sees and knows. Add here that Balaam and his donkey get into an angry and tear-jerking argument before he can continue his journey. To add to the fun, you can bring along the tales you know about hitting stubborn donkeys with two-by-fours; it's in the spirit of the story.

The prophets sometimes do odd things to declare their message. Ezekiel, for example, knocks a hole in the side of his house so he can "sneak" out, dragging his luggage behind him. Isaiah gave his sons weird names and at one point walked around Jerusalem for three years naked as witness to his message. For that matter, Jesus did things that didn't fit, like healing people in the synagogue on the Sabbath. Do you suppose that outrageous healings could be both amazing and funny all at once? And that the people who were filled with joy might grin and laugh together?

Exaggeration. Exaggeration is the powerful light-sword of humor, the magic potion that makes people laugh, the secret clue that unlocks the mysteries of the universe. It works. Comic sketch writers advise to start with something that's already funny and then to stretch it to its limits, exaggerate it as far as you can. Create images bigger than life, push toward the preposterous and absurd. In visual caricature of faces, artists choose notable features—a large nose, a receding chin, a toothy smile—and then make them larger, more receding, or toothier. Storytellers can do the same thing with characters (or caricatures) in their stories.

Exaggerating, or hyperbole, can be a way of telling the truth. Sometimes people hardly notice a problem, for example, until you make it bigger than life and make them laugh. And if your exaggeration is big enough and good enough, they won't mistake your monstrosity for the real thing, they won't take it literally. Except for sometimes they do. Jesus once taught that if your eye or your hand is leading you to hell, you should tear it out or cut if off and throw it away. I'll bet he even used grand gestures and that his audience laughed. They knew the truth under the laugh; they got it. Yet we have far too many stories of people who have taken Jesus' great joke literally and far too many offending body parts littering the ground. Literalists are littering, missing the point and the humor. Of course, not everything is an exaggeration, but wise readers need to know that some things are and to learn how to discern the difference.

Jesus develops many of his story characters as caricatures. Think of the desperate neighbor banging on your door at midnight, the woman badgering the judge, the servant forgiven an impossible debt shaking down his buddy for five bucks, or the Pharisee praying to be seen in public. In storytelling, sometimes just using oversize numbers and images, without having to decide whether they're literal or not, can add humor to the telling. Judge Ehud thrust his sword into a spectacularly fat king. Nebuchadnezzar was so mad that his face was twisted up and he ordered the furnace to be stoked to seven times hotter than usual. Jesus warned critical folks to take the log out of their own eye.

"Is that normal?" One of my students captured the spirit and overlap of these cues to humor with a brilliantly simple question. As you're reading, she said, ask, "Is that normal?" I find that keeping this question in mind often helps sniff out surprises and abrupt reversals, characters and storylines that don't fit, and exaggerations of all sorts. It also guards against the oblivious reading of the Bible that blocks our noticing the odd and outrageous.

"Imagine them smiling." I owe another student for this simple cue. She discovered it when she was trying to explain to a friend why we don't need to think Jesus was a jerk when he balked at healing the daughter of a Canaanite woman (see Matthew 15:21–28; Mark 7:24–30). Jesus first ignores the woman's plea and then says, "It is not fair to take the children's food and throw it to the dogs." Some folks seize on this reply to show that Jesus was truly human, that he could be as rotten and racist as any of us, that he had a learning curve in love.

Elton Trueblood and other interpreters think that seeing Jesus as chauvinistic and rude here is an "insufferable hypothesis" (*Humor of Christ*, 116–25). They insist that we also have to note the woman's witty reply, "Yes, Lord, yet even the dogs eat the crumbs that fall from their master's table," and see in their exchange a loving and playful banter. Without reporting detailed interpretive journeys through this text and its broader context, my friend captured the spirit of it in a phrase, "Imagine them smiling."

I've tried since to imagine smiling in many other stories. Recognizing Jesus smiling is flat-out hard for folks who rarely see pictures of Jesus as warm, happy, or friendly. But I find it helpful to wonder whether Jesus was bantering with the Samaritan woman he met at the well. I think Jesus teased a bit, maybe with a wink and a smile, when he said, "If you parents, as bad as you are ['who are evil'], know how to give good gifts to your children, how much more will your Father in heaven give good gifts to those who ask him" (slightly adapted Matthew 7:11). If you think it's possible that Jesus actually did smile, you might try that out in other conversations and encounters in the Gospels.

I've played with "Imagine them smiling" in other contexts, too. We tend to think of the prophets as yelling and scolding most of the time, but we've seen hard messages delivered with smiles and even touches of humor. Consider Elijah on Mt. Carmel wisecracking about the god Baal and his prophets. I can imagine Isaiah delivering satire pieces with a full-body grin, great timing, and pauses for audience laughter. I've wondered, too, whether we have to read the "whirlwind speeches" in Job as God relentlessly roaring at Job. I've read them aloud that way, but have since wondered whether the words might speak just as powerfully if we could hear some playful tweaking or sarcasm in them. "Tell me, Job, where were you when I laid the foundations of the earth? . . . Do you know when the mountain goats give birth? . . . Do you think you could land Leviathan with a fishhook?" Do you really think Job would miss the point if God weren't yelling? I'm still exploring with "Imagine them smiling," and I invite you to see where it might help you.

Satire. Here we enter rough and ambiguous territory. An Oxford dictionary defines satire as "the use of humor, irony, exaggeration, or ridicule to expose and criticize people's stupidity or vices." Other words or phrases often associated with satire include "aggressive," "laugh at, not with," "parody," "taunt," "lampoon," and "mock." Those features lead to a couple of problems in using and recognizing satire.

One problem is that people may not think it's funny. When readers get caught off guard by a harsh satirical attack, some folks think that it's too mean to be funny. Others will laugh and understand that the humor intensifies the attack and helps make the point. In my personal practice I try to avoid mean-spirited humor, but I think I have to side more with those who see that humor helps make satire work. In fact, sometimes humor can help you say things that you dare not say directly. It both softens and sells a message.

Another problem with satire is that often people don't get it; they take it at face value, sometimes at their peril. Now and again, for example, a congressman or other prominent leader will misread a satirical piece from *The Onion* or Andy Borowitz as a factual report, become alarmed, and issue an urgent public statement attacking it. I always wish that his handlers had whispered in his ear, "It's satire, sir. Calm down, it's comedy." He might stay mad, even for good reasons, but at least they would have spared him the embarrassment of being exposed as humor-impaired. Of course, you don't have to be a public figure to miss the satire and miss the point. We all do better when we get it.

The Bible uses satire, sometimes bold and hilarious. One of my favorite examples is in Isaiah 14, which in Hebrew identifies itself as a *mashal* on the king of Babylon. Various versions translate *mashal* as "satire," "taunt," or "song of scorn." This song is long, bitter, and funny, relishing the comeuppance (or takedownance) of a powerful and arrogant king as he enters the world of the dead, but I'll let you discover its treasures. Sadly, humor-impaired interpreters have read this in quite different ways.

In Judges 9, Jotham tells a satirical fable to attack his brother Abimelech, who has violently made himself king in Shechem. (He has killed his other sixty-nine brothers.) Jotham shouts out the fable from the top of a hill overlooking Shechem below and then high-tails it out of there before his brother can try, again, to kill him. As Marion Shutter observes, "For in that day, as in every subsequent age, there was no room for a satirist in the kingdom of an incompetent ruler" (*Wit and Humor*, 30). Which reminds me of the high risks of being a court jester. Life insurance must cost them a bundle.

Dark humor. We know that storytellers and film-makers sometimes will throw a vignette of humor into a serious or dark story. It may briefly release the tension or it may even deepen the darkness of the scene. We may welcome such vignettes or we may find them awkward or out of place. In any event, in the Bible we find bits of humor in odd places. Dark stories may include comical bits, or the humor itself may have a darkness of its own. To see it, we'll need to think again of first tellers and hearers.

The story of Judah and Tamar in Genesis 38 offers an example. In the main storyline, Judah has cheated his daughter-in-law and put her at risk socially and economically. Two of Judah's sons have been married to Tamar but died before leaving any offspring. In accord with the Israelite practice of levirate marriage, Judah has promised that she can marry a younger son when he grows up, but, out of fear, he hasn't carried through. So Tamar takes things into her own hands. When she learns that Judah is traveling, she beats him to his destination and disguises herself as a prostitute. Judah falls for it and they negotiate a price. When he seems flat out of money, she asks for his staff, cord, and personal seal, which is a bit like leaving your credit card. They can clearly identify him, but he's eager to consummate the deal. You can decide whether you think the trickster theme here is funny, but humorous bits follow.

When Judah sends a friend to pay the bill and get his stuff back, the friend asks where to find the "cult prostitute," not an ordinary hooker, apparently trying to add a bit of sophistication to the hook-up. The local folks say there is no such person around there. Later, when Tamar turns up pregnant (it worked!!), people tell Judah that she has "played the whore," and he responds, "Bring her out, and let her be burned." Now Tamar plays her hand. "The owner of this staff, cord, and seal made me pregnant." Gotcha! Adding to the irony, Tamar has twin boys, giving her sons in Judah's lineage, one of whom, Perez, became an ancestor to King David. Wrongdoing abounds in this story, and though the humor adds to the telling, it doesn't diminish its serious purpose.

Sometimes we make jokes about awkward or embarrassing subjects. In that spirit, I think the Bible includes humor about circumcision, certainly not every joke that's ever been told about circumcision, but a few. You'll get to read how murderous Saul agreed to let David marry his daughter if he would bring the king a bagful of Philistine foreskins. In his letter to the Galatians, in his warnings about false teaching, Paul says to tell the Judaizing circumcisors "I would like to see the knife slip" (5:12, *Jerusalem Bible*). Translations vary, the wise-crack remains. Paul reminds us here and elsewhere how you can be mad and funny at the same time.

Dark humor and circumcision come together in the early story about the rape of Dinah (Genesis 34). Rape begins a very ugly story, one that doesn't show up much in preaching and teaching. The rape is not funny at all. It never is. The story of double-crossing the perpetrator's clan in vicious retaliation can be. Dinah's brothers, Jacob's sons, want revenge on neighboring Prince Shechem, who has raped their sister. So they deceitfully enter into an agreement with his clan, the Hivites. Jacob's people and Shechem's people can intermarry and interweave their lives, but on the condition that all of the Hivite men will be circumcised. Shechem talks them into it, "These people are friendly with us . . . ." Then, "On the third day, when they were still in pain," two of Jacob's sons attacked the Hivite city and "killed all the males." Now this is an awful story, and the Bible itself records Jacob's strong disapproval. But I can't imagine that Israelite men could stifle their laughter about besting their enemies by tricking them into circumcision. And I've seen modern readers, sometimes slightly embarrassed, laugh, too.

You're likely to see humor in still more unexpected places if you can imagine it's possible. It might be in a Jewish maiden carrying a Greek general's head in her handbag, or Esther's cleverness under the threat of genocide, or Solomon trying to mediate a dispute between two women over a baby. In the New Testament, Jesus slipping through the traps of the Pharisees or Paul escaping murderous crowds may show funny touches as well.

The cues about the feathers and flight of humor can help you catch sight of humor in the Bible. Look for surprise, funny-fit, and exaggeration. Try "Is this normal?" to put you on alert. Experiment with where you can see smiles. Wonder whether you might see funny pieces tucked into unlikely places, like dark stories. People may name still other forms of humor: wit, irony, riddles, ridicule, repartee, and more. But with these few in hand, you have a simple field guide for your explorations.

4.

What If You Find It?

So what if you do find humor in the Bible? (Congratulations!) Then what? What do you do with it? How does that shape your understanding? Well, first of all, just laugh. Speakers and writers use humor for lots of reasons, but they always want to get a laugh, a smile or a snicker, a giggle or a guffaw. So just laugh. Even if you're grumpy or way too serious, play along a little. Enter in. At the same time, don't let laughter dismiss or trivialize texts where you see humor. It's usually up to something.

Second, when you find humor, give yourself credit for taking a first step toward understanding. Asking what you do with it is exactly the right question. It's the question you fail to ask if you don't see the humor. Skilled Bible readers ask early on what kind of literature they're dealing with—what type of story or prophetic message or wisdom saying or song or poem. Knowing that humor is involved helps us get what's going on in a text.

Third, after you've laughed and patted yourself on the back, then begin to ask, "Why is this here? What is it doing? How does it work?" Remember that humor does all kinds of good work. It may draw people in and capture their attention. It might make a story more interesting, compelling, or memorable. It might be drawing people along, getting them to smile and nod their heads, as it moves toward the heart of the message. Or it might—FLASH-BOOM!!—deliver the message. So ask: Is it trying to hammer home a point? Is it trying to soften the edges of a hard teaching so people can hear it? (Sing along now: "A spoonful of sugar helps the medicine go down.") Is it sneaking around defenses to get into the back door of the brain or the heart? Or is it serving one or more of the other uses of humor we'll note below?

As you ask these questions, let humor do its work. Let it be what it is. Don't try to fix it or improve it. Some bits of humor are hard to improve. Think of when Jesus said, "Why do you see the splinter that's in your brother's or sister's eye, but don't notice the log in your own eye?" (CEB). How are you going to improve on that? It's direct, vivid, compact, memorable. And funny! Sure, Jesus added a few words to it, using the same image, but this easily bests earnest explanations like, "Temper your criticism of others because you have blind spots and faults of your own, blah, blah." Think, too, of Jesus' quick-hit zinger, "You strain out a gnat but swallow a camel!" You could point out, I suppose, what Jesus' audience already knew, that rule-keeping Pharisees would regard a camel as unclean food, as much as a gnat. But apart from that, you mostly need to just admire the zinger and maybe play with it a bit to harvest a few extra laughs. I think it would be hard to preach a whole sermon on either of these comic bits without just mucking things up (which is not to say that it hasn't been done).

Then you have the fixes that come from literalism, from not getting the humor at all. We've already noted that literalists who heard Jesus say to tear out your eye or cut off your hand might have left the hillside of the Sermon on the Mount littered with unholy body parts. (Imagine the trouble that might stir up for tourism in modern Galilee!) Jesus' teaching about a camel going through the eye of a needle has suffered similar torture from literalists who don't get Jesus' camel humor. Medieval commentators introduced the notion that Jerusalem had some small city gates that required camels to kneel to get through them. (It didn't.) Along the way I've seen speculation about how you could spin a camel's fur into yarn so that it could be threaded through a needle, a hard task indeed. But interpretive schemes like these miss entirely how Jesus used exaggeration to get a laugh and make a point. Frederick Buechner gets much closer when he writes of "the kind of joke Jesus told when he said it is harder for a rich person to enter Paradise than for a Mercedes to get through a revolving door" (*Telling the Truth*, 63).

Writers often use humor to make a connection with readers. Playful storytelling or descriptions can help listeners identify, saying "Yeah, that's right, that's exactly the way it is, " or "I know that person," or even, "Hey, that's me, that's the way I am." Humor helps show the muddle we are as humans, full of contradictions and paradox, resplendent with great powers and silly failures. Being able to laugh and own our funny mix can lead to helpful learning.

Some connections can even open the way for tweaking or teasing. We know, for example, that Paul knew the Christians at Corinth very well. He had lived among them and taught them, and they wrote to him seeking advice about problems in their common life. In his first letter to them, Paul gets after them right away for picking sides about who baptized them and for getting uppity with each other. Perhaps he's both teaching and teasing a bit when he says, "At least no one can go around saying he was baptized in my name" (except maybe that one family) (1 Corinthians 1:15–16, *The Message*).

Paul goes on to talk about the foolishness of the gospel and how God had chosen to show power and wisdom through the weak and foolish. To drive the point home, it seems to me, he tweaks his friends at Corinth directly: "Take a good look, friends, at who you were when you got called into this life. I don't see many of 'the brightest and the best' among you. . . .God deliberately chose 'nobodies.' . . . [So] none of you can get by with blowing your own horn before God . . ." (1:26–29, *The Message*). Yes, imagine him smiling, getting some giggles, and making his point stick.

When Jesus fed the 5,000, I imagine he had some fun with his disciples in the process. They had asked Jesus to send the hungry crowd away so they could get something to eat. Jesus' first response left the disciples slack-jawed and sputtering. "You feed them," he said (Luke 9:13). After laughing through their "But . . . but . . . we can't do that," Jesus showed them how to get on with the meal. What a joyful day!

Where we have repeated exposures to someone like Samson or David, humor can help create a fuller picture of the person. Funny stories that show how clever, playful, or mischievous they were complement stories about wisdom or valor. My students discovered that seeing Jesus as sometimes funny or playful made him more accessible to them. Humorous words directly from Jesus, Paul, or others also give glimpses of their character, again deepening our understanding. Happily, once we see that they might actually have a sense of humor, it keeps us alert to where they might have used it. It makes it easier to "imagine them smiling."

Sometimes biblical writers also used humor to characterize, more likely to caricature, oppressors or enemies. For example, in the story of the judge Ehud's sneaky victory over the king of Moab, the writer makes sure that readers know that the king is fat and that both the king and his personal bodyguards are stupid. Whatever you make of it, people still use fat and stupid as comic slurs on their foes. In another instance, the story of David's encounter with Nabal ("Fool") shows repeatedly how fully Nabal lives up to his name.

Sometimes humor serves to illustrate a teaching point. Paul, for example, uses the analogy of the church as the Body of Christ in Romans, 1 Corinthians, and Ephesians. But in 1 Corinthians 12, he playfully elaborates the image to make sure his readers catch on. Pointing out that all members of the body are important, he asks fun, absurd questions like, "Suppose the whole body were an eye?" And here we need to slow down and not just blow by the text. We need to read with imagination and to picture the text. It's quite fun to visualize a monstrously large and lonely eye or ear. Purposefully and playfully, Paul explores the importance of feet, hands, weak parts, and even what we do with the "least honorable" parts. Paul used humor, I suspect, partly because he could with these Corinthian friends (we see other examples) and partly because he had some hard-headed folks in the mix that humor might reach.

Another way writers use humor is to make obvious the ridiculous and the absurd. These are the-king-has-no-clothes moments, and comical exaggeration creates them. Sadly, we are easily numbed by nonsense and by hurtful practice, especially when spinmeisters work their magic. So sometimes we need a comic jolt to jar us back to reality. One example is Isaiah's sharp satire about the man who cut down a tree he had grown, used half of it to warm the house and bake bread, carved an idol out of the other half, and then prayed to it, "Save me. You are my god." Isaiah goes on, "This guy didn't have the wit to say . . . 'What I have in my hand is nothing but a lie'" (Isaiah 44:9–20).

Perhaps Jesus used a similar approach in telling about an outrageously successful farmer who kept building bigger and bigger barns and who was smugly confident that he had things under control, that he was set for life (Luke 12:16–21). The story's abrupt end, the farmer's abrupt end, surely evoked gasps and giggles.

Ridiculous, absurd stories that make us laugh can also bear witness to grace. The Bible has lots of them. God chooses the most unlikely people ("Who me? Do what?") as heroes and uses weird, even funny, means to deliver folks. Even as Abraham and Sarah were cackling at the prospect that in old age they would have the child of promise, we have the phrase, "Is anything too wonderful for God?" (Genesis 18:14). God's action among us can be outsized, amazing, unexpected, and so extraordinary that we laugh with wonder and tears of joy. Perhaps, as Frederick Buechner suggests, "the [g]ospel itself [is] the highest and holiest joke of them all. . . . Is it possible, I wonder, to say that it is only when you hear the [g]ospel as a wild and marvelous joke that you really hear it at all? Heard as anything else, the [g]ospel is the church's thing, the preacher's thing, the lecturer's thing. Heard as a joke—high and unbidden and ringing with laughter—it can only be God's thing" (*Telling the Truth*, 63, 68).

A brief, but important aside: even if you have a fabulous sense of humor, you may find humor in the Bible that you don't think is funny. That is, the writers clearly intended humor, but it bothers you. That happens to me, too. Of course, it's not just with the Bible; for me it happens with some modern humor, too. For years now I have tried to shape my humor to the principle, "Laugh with others as you would have them laugh with you." Obviously that excludes some common practices in humor—insult humor, name-calling, us-versus-them category humor (ethnic, gender, nationalistic, etc.), some satire—and these practices seem less funny to me than they used to, even when the Bible uses them. (I explore this nearly "golden" principle in some detail in my book *Laughing Pilgrims: Humor and the Spiritual Journey*.) So you may rightly identify places the Bible uses humor, but you might not laugh. That's okay. It's still useful to see humor at work.

No doubt you'll discover still other ways that the Bible uses humor. That's the happy fruit of your exploring where the humor is and wondering what it's doing there. I'd love to know what you find, but all the while I'll be cheering for you and those with you who undertake this journey of discovery.

II.

Field Guides for Explorers

WHENEVER I SET OUT on an adventure to explore a new area, to watch birds, to take photographs, or to go fishing, I'm always glad to have some tips about where to look and what to look for. I often look to guidebooks and experienced guides to suggest promising routes and hot spots. Maybe you do, too. So as you explore humor in the Bible, here are some field guides to help you.

Each of these field guides has an introduction and then a series of texts you can scout to see what you discover. Our goal is to leave the fun of discovery to you. At the same time, the guides offer background information, links, and hints to help you succeed. These guides include a wide array of biblical texts, though they're not exhaustive. We've left plenty of texts for you to find on your own.

Bring along your best tools. Use translations that sound like the ordinary English that you speak (well, maybe not *that* English). Read spaciously and imaginatively, using all your senses. Don't be in a hurry. Enter the scene, experimenting with reading aloud or portraying the action. Review, if you wish, what we've said earlier about how to read. Jotting notes about what I discover or questions I have helps me to learn. Others learn by doodling, drawing, or using other creative responses. See what works for you.

You can embark on this exploration on your own, of course, and I hope you'll learn and laugh a lot. Depending on whether and how you share a household, you might have to be discreet (though hopefully not secretive), especially if you experiment with loud or silly voices or vigorously act out stone-throwing or sword-play. On the other hand, your housemates, adults or kids, might be curious and would even be glad to join in some of the fun. Do be careful with swords and stones.

What's even more fun, in my experience, is to read and journey with others. It could be a group of curious friends (don't we all have some curious friends?), a reading or Bible study group, or even a class. (This is a book I wish I could have used in teaching biblical interpretation or "Humor and the Bible.") As you can, find ways to share your joy in learning.

The Founding Family

GENESIS 12–38

The stories of Israel's founding families offer rich detail and many links between the individual pieces. Taken together, the stories carry the themes of how God acted faithfully, often against the odds, and of how the various characters walked or wavered in their own faithfulness.

Quite a few of the stories also offer humor, whether through absurdity, trickery, surprises, or the challenges of sibling rivalry. Of course, you don't really want to refer to forbears in the family of faith as liars and cheats, but both Abraham and Isaac tried to pass their wives off as their sisters. And the ways Jacob and Laban made deals with each other might make you cringe. Maybe another large theme of these stories can be "what goes around comes around."

More than in some other sections we'll examine, the best practice to see the humor in individual stories is to read to get the whole flow of the narratives. That way you can have at hand the various characterizations and relationships on which some of the later stories build. To help you explore, though, I'll break the storyline into episodes and offer some clues or cross-references.

Genesis 12:10–20. Hot "sisters"

Right after God's grand promises to him, Abraham acts to help God come through. After all, it's hard to be the father of a great nation if you starve to death or if Pharaoh kills you. Or, as readers know, if the mother of the great nation winds up in Pharaoh's harem. So Abraham's trickery begins with smooth words to Sarah (12:11–12). He wisely avoided saying, "Dear, you don't look a day over eighty."

See also *Genesis 20:1–18*. *"What were you thinking?"*

Back in Canaan, where Abraham's semi-nomadic clan deals with local city-states ruled by kings. Of course, Abraham wants to get off to a good start.

And *Genesis 26:7–11. Subtlety subverted*

In verse 8, translations range from "laughing together" to "caressing" or "fondling" to "making love." Maybe Isaac didn't have the savvy to pull off the big lie.

Genesis 17:15–22; 18:1–15; 21:1–7, The birth of "He Laughs" (Isaac, Yitzhak)

These three stories give neon notice that God's work (and the Bible) will include laughter. We don't need to add our own wonderings about geriatric maternity fashion here. A footnote alternative translation of Genesis 21:6 adds to the mix: "God has made a joke of me. Everyone who hears about it will laugh at me" (CEB).

Genesis 18:16–33. Bargaining with God

The topic is serious, but the conversation could remind folks of what they dread about buying a car.

Genesis 25:29–34. Soup traps hunter

The account of Esau and Jacob's birth (Genesis 25:19–26) sets up the conflict stories that follow. Esau, the firstborn of the twins, had special rights of inheritance, as long as he retained the "birthright" and received his father's death-bed blessing. In this story and the next, Jacob plots to get them both.

Genesis 27:1-45. The game of blessing

No doubt some days Isaac felt like death warmed over. He couldn't see well, and probably in his old age his hearing, his taste buds, and his touch were failing, too. No wonder he wanted to give Esau his "death-bed blessing" while he still could. And he loved Esau's wild game cooking.

Jacob reluctantly cooperates in his mother's what-could-possibly-go-wrong scheme. (Note: a bit of created humor here, but realistic. "Mom, Esau is hairy, but really?!) The scenes are awkward, awful, and sometimes funny. Slow down and use your senses.

Genesis 29:15-30. Two for the price of two

Esau answered his family's betrayal, in part, by marrying women they would hate (Genesis 28:6-9; 36:1-5). To quote Rebekah: "I really loathe these Hittite women" (27:46). Jacob, on the other hand, was glad to escape with his life and set out to Haran, following his parents' instructions, to marry one of the daughters of his Uncle Laban. Cousin Rachel turned out to be the girl of his dreams. But you do marry family, and Jacob should have known better than to trust Uncle Laban (his mother's brother) so much. Also note an enduring practical tip: always look first under the veil.

Genesis 29:31—30:24. True love and baby wars

Women in my classes taught me a lot when they caught the humor here so quickly. Guys can be slow sometimes. (Women get that, too.) But the women had sisters, knew sisters, and knew well how sister rivalry and fighting can be. So they understood right away competing for love, the baby derby, and the symbolic naming. (Some translations and study Bibles include notes explaining the babies' names. Knowing that sharpens the story.)

The *Common English Bible* helpfully translates "erotic herbs" in 30:14 to speak of "mandrakes." Knowing the plants are aphrodisiacs boosts our understanding.

Genesis 30:25–43. Let's make a deal

Jacob wants to go home; Laban wants him to stay. After all, Laban prospers with Jacob around. Enjoy the twists and turns in bargaining and behavior. The story reminds me to watch out when a wheeler-dealer says, "I will be completely honest with you" (30:33).

Genesis 31:1–35. The almost-great escape

"Jacob saw that Laban no longer liked him as much as he used to" (31:2). Neither did his sons. It's time to leave. But making a clean getaway takes planning and stealth. Rachel eagerly joined in by secretly stealing her father's small household idols ("teraphim"), often thought to give her economic advantage.

It takes Laban ten days to overtake Jacob's caravan, but when he does, he gives what must be one of the greatest sob speeches of all time. Then the storyteller dazzles us in describing Laban's search, full of suspense and humor as it narrows to the secret villain. Apparently vindicated, Jacob matches Laban with sob and outrage of his own (31:36–42).

Genesis 31:43–54. One last deal: a treaty

In the "Christian Endeavor" groups of my youth, we often concluded our meetings with these words of blessing and tenderness: "The Lord watch between me and thee, when we are absent one from another" (31:49, KJV). This last scuffle between Laban and Jacob conveys a different tone. The gods of both men, the God of Nahor and the God of Abraham, are called to witness and guarantee their agreement.

Genesis 33:1–17. A clumsy, cautious reunion

How do you meet the brother you cheated and fled years ago? The awkward, warm, and wary moments can bring smiles.

Genesis 38. Tamar's gamble

When Judah says of Tamar, "She's more righteous than I am" (38:26), he doesn't offer either of their actions as model behaviors.

It's a troublesome story, but as we've suggested in others, it uses humor in the telling.

One thread is Judah trying to cover up what he's done. He sends a friend to pay off the "prostitute" (the Hebrew uses the ordinary word for hooker), but on arriving, the friend asks for the "cult prostitute" or "holy woman" (CEB), a more respected role in Canaanite culture.

The great "gotcha" thread is the deposit Tamar required for credit for services rendered. Judah's signature seal, cord, and staff would identify him as distinctly as a credit card would today. What a moment when she uses them!

This story is here, in part, to show that Perez, one of the twins born of Judah's tryst, becomes an ancestor of King David and of Jesus (Matthew 1:3).

Humor in the Stories about Joseph

Genesis 37, 39–48

Joseph had a lot going for him. He was the firstborn of Rachel, his father's favorite wife. So he got special treatment as Jacob's favorite son. He was "well-built and handsome." (39:6) And smart, though early on with some adolescent naiveté. With these advantages, though, he had a roller-coaster life, hurtling from high points to low to high.

The storytellers of Genesis present Joseph's story artfully, developing themes like high-to-low and double-dreams as they go. They also include themes and extended passages of humor. Chapter 37 sets the stage well for the theme of sibling rivalry and family bickering. One of my favorite examples is when, after he has rescued his brothers, Joseph sends them back toward Canaan with, "Now just try to get along" (45:24). Trickery shows up a lot in the stories, not surprisingly, given the history of this family. I chuckled when his brothers, keeping a straight face, told the Egyptian governor (Joseph), "We are honest men" (42:10). And there are a lot of reversals and turning things upside-down. If you jot down notes as you read, you may well be surprised at how many funny bits you'll see.

Humor in Judges

In the centuries before the Hebrews had a king and a centralized government, they were led by "judges." These leaders had administrative and judicial roles, but the book of Judges tells us mostly about how they delivered the Israelites from their enemies, whether marauding tribes or next-door neighbors.

The stories of the judges often include humorous elements and sometimes feel like folklore sagas. In one way or another, the judges themselves were unlikely heroes, among the least likely to succeed. They rescue Israel with out-of-the-blue strategies, packed with surprises and reversals. Sometimes they're sneaky, sometimes strong, and often filled with daring and mischief. As you read, try to enter into the delight Israel's storytellers would enjoy in sharing these remarkable accounts.

Judges 3:12–30. Tricky lefty

Even now left-handed folks know what it means to be disregarded. Our words "sinister" and "gauche" come from the long negative treatment of lefties. Adding to the fun of this story is that Ehud is from the tribe of Benjamin, which means "son of a right hand."

Note the several trickster elements and the ways the story uses the old comic slur that presents enemies as fat and stupid. (Yes, I know it's a gory story, too. Even if I prefer otherwise, in these stories of violent conflict, guts and guffaws often show up together.)

Judges 4:17–22. Good with a gavel

Jael was neither a "judge" nor an Israelite, though her treacherous hospitality helped secure an Israelite victory. (In Judges 5:24–30, Deborah's victory song recalls both Jael's action and poignant words showing Sisera's mother waiting for his return.)

Judges 6:11–24. Valiant warrior

Heroes in the Bible often respond to God's call with "Who me? Do what?" The irony of the setting of this call makes it even more fun. Gideon's actions and his cheeky give-and-take not only make us chuckle but may also remind us of ourselves. ("I'm no hero. I'm just a poor boy from a tiny clan . . . .")

Judges 6:25–32. Courage in the dark

God directs Gideon to do something dangerous; after all, people don't like you messing with their true religion, in this case, Canaanite religion. But Gideon was courageous, sort of. Maybe his father was even more so, "Let Baal argue for himself."

Judges 6:33–40. Fleecing God

"The Lord's spirit came over Gideon." This is calling and empowerment. But you can't be too sure.

Judges 7:1–8a. Thinning the troops

The enemy was too numerous to count (7:12). But Gideon had too many volunteers. With the first cut, two-thirds of them left. The next cut reduced the army to impossible odds, just the right size. The methods to thin the ranks are fun.

Judges 7:8b–15. Eavesdropping for courage

And take your servant.

Judges 7:15–22. Shofar so good

Enjoy the unusual strategy using "trumpets" (*shofar*) made from animal horns. Try to picture the middle-of-the-night chaos in the camp.

Judges 9:1–21. King Thorn

One of Gideon's sons, Abimelech ("My father is king"), uses bloody brute force to be made king at Shechem. The one brother who escapes his sword stands on the hill just above the city to shout out a scathing satire in the form of a fable. The trees and shrubs in the fable make the case. Then Jotham hightails it to escape Abimelech's reach.

Judges 13. The messenger's surprise

The story of Samson's birth amuses readers throughout. Start with the messenger's abrupt announcement to the barren woman. Continue through the meetings and conversations with the messenger. Manoah can't quite figure out who this figure is until just before he exclaims, "We're going to die."

Perhaps a note about translation will help here. The Hebrew word for "messenger," *mal'ak*, is also often translated as "angel." (See also with Gideon in Judges 6:12.) Sadly, modern readers too easily think of wings and chubby butts, so it's charming but misleading. In this story we see change and mystery. The woman tells her husband that a "man of God" came to her, and that he looked like "a *mal'ak* of God," an appearance or presence that seemed "very awesome" or "scary." Yet as the story goes on we see the terms "man," "man of God," and all the way to "*mal'ak* of the Lord (YHWH)."

Judges 14. A woman caught my eye

The stories in the next several chapters leave a lot of loose ends for folks who like to keep theology and Bible reading tidy. The big bundle Samson, with his out-sized feats and naughty ventures, overwhelms any easy sense of tidy. These folk-hero stories stir up childhood memories of hearing about John Bunyan and Pecos

Bill. Like them, Samson is bigger than life. He's strong and smart enough to outwit and outfight any foe and to overcome any obstacle . . . except, sometimes, a femme fatale and flashes of stupidity.

The stories and conversations that come from the woman at Timnah catching Samson's eye provide great examples. The pleading and crying episode plays out a stock scene in comedy.

Judges 15. How about her sister?

These are out-sized, ugly, dirty-trick stories, maybe not great for kids. Yet I suspect the Israelites laughed as they told how Samson bested their enemies, the Philistines. (Occasionally I hear people who know this story use the phrase "the jawbone of an ass" to refer to particularly obnoxious public speakers.)

Judges 16:1–3. The gates of Gaza

Another woman caught Samson's eye, and the Philistines thought they had him. As you read, remember that the doors of Gaza's walled city were huge. And imagine Samson carrying them forty miles uphill to Hebron overnight.

Judges 16:4–22. If you really loved me . . . .

Finally Delilah, another Philistine beauty, but this one he "loved," the Bible says. Most of the chapter is dialogue, full of pleading, teasing, lying, and, no doubt, crying. Imagine the give-and-take, the fluttering eyelashes, the tone of voice. Even better, read it aloud expressively with mostly man and woman voices, trimming the narrator to only what's necessary. (You won't need "he/she said.") Embarrass yourself with exaggeration, and giggle.

Judges 16:23–31. Bringing down the house

Apart from my lame pun, in what ways do you think the Hebrew hearers might find this funny?

Humor about David: Hero on the Run

With his improbable defeat of Goliath and other early military success, David instantly became a folk hero, stirring up King Saul's suspicion and hostility. Surely stories about this young hero raced through families and villages, and some of them survive to us today.

Apparently you could tell funny stories about David before he became king, but not about David as king. 1 Samuel puts humorous touches on lots of stories about David's giant-felling, his close calls and derring-do, and his cunning and knowing naiveté. I've seen less fun in 2 Samuel. Maybe it's easier to show humor in stories about David as folk hero than David as king.

1 Samuel 16:1–13. Is this all you have?

Now that Samuel has twice rejected Saul as king, God sends him to choose ("anoint") a new one. That proves scary and tricky. Note Eliab, Jesse's firstborn and apparently the pick of the litter. He shows up again later.

1 Samuel 17:(12–22)23–31. David curious about Goliath

With care packages from home, David also brought curiosity and brash courage: "Who does this Philistine think he is?!" Eliab, who watched his kid brother get anointed, has had enough.

1 Samuel 17:32–39. Bravado and clunky armor

David's "Oh-yes-I-can" speech is endearing, at least, in response to Saul noting the obvious. When you picture the armor-fitting scene, remember that Saul "was head and shoulders taller" than all the Israelites. (1 Samuel 10:23)

1 Samuel 18:17–27. David marries Saul's daughter

As much as I like *The Message*, Eugene Peterson's translation "evidence" here is just too polite. The Philistine guys who provided David's sack full of "evidence" were pretty attached to it and surely resisted any tampering with the evidence, even if it was for a princess' dowry.

1 Samuel 19:8–17. Michal saves David

It hardly surprised Michal that her father still wanted to kill David, her new groom. But she loved him alive. This rescue/escape scene is classic, including her self-defense.

1 Samuel 19:18–24. Saul among the prophets

1 Samuel 9:26—10:16 tells a similar story. In this instance note that murderous rage overcomes risk assessment.

1 Samuel 21:10–15. Feigning madness at Gath

At Philistine Gath, King Achish's servants identified David right away, but wrongly. He wasn't the king of Israel; he was running from the king of Israel. But it put David in peril. After David's and Achish's responses, it's amusing to see David as one of Achish's trusted military leaders. (1 Samuel 27)

1 Samuel 24:1–15(–22). David spares Saul

So with plenty of caves to choose from, why would Saul pick the one you're hiding in to enter and "cover his feet" (KJV), a euphemism for "taking a powder," if that's what he was doing? It amuses me to imagine David sneaking up on him. It's funnier still to think his not-so-genteel band of guerilla warriors could stifle their laughter to remain stealthy.

1 Samuel 25. The grumpy fool

You need to know that Nabal's name means "fool," mostly because the story shows how he lives up to his name. An amazing ranch woman reminded me that on farm and ranch, the first step toward resolving conflict is serving food. Some interpreters speculate about the medical condition that killed Nabal, but to me the Bible's words are just fine.

1 Samuel 26 David spares Saul (again)

Sneaky moves against the odds. And some trash-talking.

(If you're real enthusiastic about this you might also consider 1 Samuel 21:1–9; 1 Samuel 28:3–25.)

Humor in the Early Prophets

Israel often told stories to remember its early prophets (before 800 B.C.). Sometimes the stories describe the prophets' actions. Sometimes they recount an occasion when a prophet spoke, what he said or did, and what came of it. The outcomes serve to authenticate the power and the word of the prophet.

In looking for humor, consider both the prophetic figure and the narrator. What the prophets did, from trash-talking to surprising actions, can be funny in their own right. But sometimes the narrator arranges the stories cleverly to help us see humor.

Numbers 22:(1–21), 22–35. Chatty donkey saves the seer

The reader's question, "Is this normal?" definitely applies here unless your reality routinely includes talking animals. Using your best whiney, accusing voice, you might try reading aloud the donkey's sob story. And don't miss the rest of the fun details.

Numbers 22:36—24:25. How hard can it be to get a curse?

Israel believed that real prophets spoke only the message God gave them. You couldn't pay a true prophet a big fee to get the message you want. You could hire a phony, as Jeremiah and Ezekiel complain that Israel often did, but you only fool yourself.

1 Kings 18:16–39. Can I get some fire here?

After a three-year drought, Elijah and the prophets of Baal, the Canaanite storm god, compete to see whose god will bring rain.

Note the details that are bigger than life, including the ecstatic dancing and cutting themselves that Baal's prophets did to try to get some action. No doubt Elijah's sideline "encouragement" made them redouble their efforts.

1 Kings 22:1–28. *The never-good prophet*

The kings of Israel and Judah start planning to go to war against Aram (Syria) to reclaim a border town. When considering war, leaders were supposed to "seek the Lord," consult with God, about whether they should go or not. King Ahab seems ready.

2 Kings 5:1–19. *Washing in the lazy, muddy Jordan*

I hurt from laughing as my friend told the story of "Captain White Hand," the enemy general who came to Elisha to be healed of leprosy. He told the story a bit too creatively, no doubt, but the biblical writers themselves give us plenty to laugh at.

Naaman was a decorated general in Aram's army, one who had led successful raiding parties into Israel. He "was a mighty warrior, but he had a skin disease" (2 Kings 5:1 CEB). The ironies and twists and turns of the story entertain from there.

Follow with 2 Kings 5:20–27. *The self-serving servant*

Sometimes it's just wrong to spurn generosity born of gratitude. ("Just one? No, really, take two!") Elisha's servant Gehazi rises to the occasion.

2 Kings 6:1–7. *A panicked borrower*

The company of prophets who lived in community around Elisha had grown and gotten crowded. Even good solutions sometimes require a prophet as handyman.

2 Kings 6:8–23. *Eye-openers*

Dothan, where this story begins, was just ten miles north of Samaria, the capital of Israel. Clearly Aram (Syria) dominated Israel and could bring troops into the land quite easily. However, Elisha the prophet had often thwarted their plans. It's time to deal with him!

Humor in the Story about Esther
ESTHER 1–10

The Book of Esther is very fun to read. Though it includes seemingly sober themes of courage and deliverance, commentators often describe the book with words like "farce" or "hilarious," and they admire the author's masterful use of humor. (It would be fun if both the author and the heroine were women because I'm sure some of the humor in the story is a lot funnier for women than for men.)

The common devices of humor shape the story freely. Exaggeration shows up everywhere, starting with the comic excess of a six-month long feast to satisfy the king's reckless boasting. The spotlight turns next to the foibles of power and vanity as the inebriated king makes foolish decisions with counsel from his drunken smart advisors. (What do you expect when you have days and days of free royal wine from a no-limits, open bar?) The story has sudden reversals and twists in plot. Some characters have grand plans, but turn out to be clumsy and unlucky. To me, the all-powerful king seems to get pushed around pretty easily. Trickster themes occur, too, some showing the prowess of wily Queen Esther.

When Jews celebrate the Festival of Purim, leaders read aloud the story of Esther, prompting rowdy responses and laughter from the audience. They boo and stomp their feet when they hear the name of Haman, the chief villain; they cheer for heroes Mordecai and Esther; they laugh as wicked plans get thwarted. Costumes, noisemakers, food, and drink add to make it a hoot. If you want to join the carnival fun, you can easily buy Purim gear over the internet, or make your own, or pretend. But make sure to laugh.

Humor in the Wisdom Literature

Israel's wisdom tradition ranges from practical teaching about how to live well to searching conversations about life's biggest questions. The book of Proverbs collects mostly short sayings to teach people about relationships, planning well, work habits, prudence, integrity, compassion, and much more. The books of Ecclesiastes and Job lean into wondering what makes life worth living, how to think about dying, and how to make sense of suffering and mystery. We'll explore here how humor might help in the teaching and wondering of wisdom.

Proverbs grow up in virtually all cultures and they share many common traits. They're short and catchy. They use vivid images and other devices to make them memorable. Those include sharp contrasts, word-play, and humor. Translators struggle, of course, to keep the word-play of the original, though they may succeed in imitating. Happily, translations often do preserve well the ideas and humor of the original texts. So we can enjoy and learn from old and foreign proverbs, even as cultural and linguistic foreigners.

To get the impact of proverbs, you have to treat them with respect. They're short sayings, and it's easy to skim over them without enjoying the contrasts and word pictures they offer. It helps, too, to use translations that sound like the language we speak. I have found in Proverbs, especially, that Eugene Peterson's translation in *The Message* often gives the sayings more clarity and punch, sometimes changing old metaphors to something clearer. Sometimes comparing translations also help open understanding.

Discovering humor in wisdom's more contemplative books with their "big questions" seems more unlikely. I still remember how surprised I was to find an article on humor in Ecclesiastes, and the gut-wrenching questions of Job seem to demand a serious, respectful demeanor. However, even here humor can do good work. Exaggeration can still be funny. Odd contrasts, sarcasm, satire, and making fun of folly can clarify the issues or sharpen the point. I'm still experimenting to learn how being open to humor in places we don't expect might actually bring fresh, hopefully better, understanding.

Many readers regard Ecclesiastes as a pretty gloomy text, particularly when they suffer under the traditional use of the word "vanity." ("Fleeting" or "fragile" serve better for the Hebrew word *hebel*.) Part of the adventure of reading might be to imagine that someone could offer gloomy observation but do it with a humorous tone.

In Job, too, I suspect humor does its work through exaggeration in the opening narrative, through the bombastic sarcasm in the dialogues of the friends, and even in playful questioning in the "whirlwind speeches." You can explore these below.

Texts from Proverbs

>*11:22*
>*13:8*
>*17:12*
>*17:28*
>*18:6*
>*20:4*
>*20:19*
>*21:9*
>*22:3*
>*22:13*
>*27:14*
>*27:15–16*

Ecclesiastes 1:12–18. The Teacher
Ecclesiastes 5:10–12. Troubles with wealth
Ecclesiastes 10. Fun images and sayings

Most of these sayings resemble proverbs. Verse 20 always makes me laugh.

Job 1:1–5. Best man ever!

This is one of those brief resumés that you read and say, "Nobody is that good!" In the story, though, Job functions as the best guy in the history of the universe, a person of absolute integrity. It's important, but it's so over the top that it's also funny. Verses 4–5 clinch it for me (and play later in the story).

Job 13:1–12; 15:1–16; 26:1–4. Don't be an old windbag!

"Friends" hurl insults and play one-upmanship in the thick of their important conversations. It strikes me as comic relief.

Job 38–41. Serious but ridiculous questions

"Since you're so smart, here's a quiz." Right away you know it's going to be a tough session. "Let's start with laying the foundations of the earth. And how about telling me when and where the mountain goats have their young? Do you really think you'll reel in Leviathan with a fly rod?" Sometimes I've read these passages aloud with a booming, accusing voice, which is plausible. But I've wondered whether we might hear it as both challenging and playful, pointedly teasing at the edges of mystery and human limitation. You might experiment with that.

Humor in the Prophetic Books

When people look for humor in the prophetic books some see almost none, others see a lot. If we consider both how humor works and what the prophets needed to do, we should expect they would use humor as a tool.

The prophets had to grab people's attention and make their messages vivid and memorable and, as the texts suggest, even surprising or shocking. In calling their hearers to change their ways, the prophets needed to challenge complacency and fraud as well as renew encouragement and hope.

The prophets found great tools in the devices of humor. Sometimes they used exaggeration to make things look as silly, ridiculous, or dangerous as they really were. Sometimes they caricatured individuals or groups. Or they might use funny-fit by laying side by side things that looked silly together, the powers of idols alongside the power of God, for example. The prophets also used satire, which is often funny, though not always. They used language that mocked and shocked. Even when we're outraged by shocking words, sometimes we laugh and say, "I can't believe he really said that!" ("Hear this word, you cows of Bashan," Amos' words to rich women in Samaria (4:1) probably got some shocked laughter.) They even used humor that included gross-out and sexual sayings that you probably won't hear read aloud in family-friendly settings.

Israel's prophets also delivered messages through their actions, not just words, and these used humor, too. It might be a one-time act like Jeremiah burying his loincloth (think underpants, BVDs) in a riverbank and retrieving the rotted briefs later

(Jeremiah 13:1–11), or Ezekiel publicly giving himself a haircut with a sword (Ezekiel 5). It might be an extended act like Isaiah going naked for three years (Isaiah 20), or Ezekiel's months-long street theater in Jerusalem (Ezekiel 4). Or it might be a lifestyle action like Jeremiah not marrying and never going to parties or funerals (Jeremiah 16:1–9), or Ezekiel trembling while he ate and acting nervous as he drank (Ezekiel 12:17–20).

Much of the prophetic literature isn't funny at all. But the prophets used humor well and more often than we think. It's good to stay alert so we can understand them more clearly. On this adventure with the texts I keep making new discoveries, and I hope you will, too. In the passages below we've offered just samples, by no means an exhaustive list. Read spaciously. Imagine that the prophets might have spoken with playful or sarcastic tones rather than just yelling at people. Look for the sly mixed with the bold. Let smiles and laughter surprise you.

Isaiah 44:9–20. Crafting a god

A farmer-craftsman plants trees, bakes bread, and makes a god.

Jeremiah 10:1–16. Nail it down

This is another of the common satires on the folly of idols, who are prone to fall over.

Micah 6:1–8. What does God want?

In this scene God puts Israel on trial, calling witnesses and bringing charges. Micah humorously exaggerates the people's response to the charges against them. Then he adds, "This really isn't hard . . . ."

Isaiah 14:3–23. Welcome to Sheol! Happy to see you here!

The world's most powerful and feared king gets an animated welcome to Sheol, the world of the dead. He has finally met his comedownance. Satire runs rampant.

Isaiah 3:16–24. Fancy women stroll and strut

The wealthy women of Jerusalem share the guilt of those who "crush my people and grind the faces of the poor" (3:14). But crushing folks can help you fill your closets with lots of fashion and accessories. This caricature raises funny images but hardly spares its targets.

Jeremiah 27–28. The yoke's on you

A lively dispute over a yoke Jeremiah wore to prophesy.

Jeremiah 32. Do I have a deal for you!

Jerusalem is under siege, property values are tanking, and Jeremiah is in jail. What could possibly go wrong? Imagine how the prison guards and other observers must have laughed as Jeremiah buys into this deal.

Ezekiel 12:1–16. The hole in the wall

Pack a bag for exile; dig a hole in the wall. They'll watch, and maybe they'll get it.

Ezekiel 24:15–27. No tears, no mourning rites

Ezekiel's actions are stubbornly countercultural. People just didn't act this way. Many observers didn't laugh, though Ezekiel had long been a weird one. Maybe folks shook their heads, chuckled, and said, "There he goes again!"

Book of Jonah. Forgiving the worst people ever

This story of the rebellious, not just reluctant, prophet brims over with humor. Follow the twists and turns in the first chapter, including the actions and prayers of the sailors. In the third chapter, see how half-heartedly Jonah obeys his call and how wholeheartedly the Ninevites and their cattle repent. Finally, listen in on Jonah's angry conversation with God. The whole story sharply rebukes those who want to limit God's grace.

Conrad Hyers includes a wonderful chapter on Jonah in *And God Created Laughter.*

Humor in the Apocrypha

The books of the Apocrypha were written in the few centuries before the coming of Jesus. They grew out of the Jewish community of faith and they continue and develop themes that Jews had long cherished. Just as we should expect, the Apocryphal writings also include humor. Enjoy the several examples that follow.

Tobit. Do the right thing

The Book of Tobit is a story that promotes right living and adhering to basic Jewish values. The author scrambles historical detail, perhaps to let readers know that this is a historical novel. Humorous bits track through the story, including Tobit being blinded by sparrows pooping in his eyes (2:9–10), his son Tobias driving out a demon with a smelly incense odor (8:1–3), and Tobias' new father-in-law digging a grave for him on his wedding night (8:9–17). Frederick Buechner's charming novel, *On the Road with the Archangel*, is based on this story.

Judith. Head in a handbag

By using the city name Bethulia, which we know only through this story, and by mixing other historical details, the author marks this as a historical novel. The storyline and details are all grand. The opening chapters build up the mighty general Holofernes, full of victory, hubris, and bravado. Chapter 8 introduces Judith, who was astonishingly beautiful and equally smart, the Israelite woman who delivered her city from Holofernes' siege warfare. Judith's victory song says that she "paralyzed him with her beauty" (16:6), though he had other plans and she wasn't satisfied to leave him lying dead drunk in his tent. The details and dialogues of the stories are fun to read. In the end they reinforce themes of faithfulness, both by God and by Israel.

Letter of Jeremiah. Rusting, rotting gods

This is an extended collection of sharply satirical warnings (and reassurances) about the uselessness and powerlessness of idols. It's put-down humor on the loose.

Susanna. Courtroom drama

Daniel rescues lovely Susanna from the schemes of two lecherous and powerful old men. Humorous currents run through the several scenes of the story.

Bel and the Dragon 1–22. "God" with an appetite

In a high-stakes challenge about what the king's "god" eats, trickery overcomes trickery. Bel (or "Marduk") is the chief god of Babylon.

Bel and the Dragon 23–27. Exploding dragons

Daniel's recipe to expose false gods. You may have to experiment with proportions.

Bel and the Dragon 28–32. Eating between the lions

Another story of Daniel thrown to the hungry lions. It features abrupt reversals and Habakkuk's quick round-trip hair travel.

Introduction to Jesus' Use of Humor

Whether or not we can see humor in Jesus' life and teaching depends a lot on how we think of Jesus as a character. On the one hand, seeing him as a perpetual man of sorrows clouds any hint of humor, as does imagining Jesus as always serious, overly earnest, or even grumpy. Some Jesus films actually do that, and the great preponderance of visual art in the church barely hints otherwise.

On the other hand, we might see Jesus as usually joyful, even playful, as an engaging storyteller, witty, and a keen observer of our common humanity with all its quirkiness, mess-ups, and flaws. If we can't imagine that Jesus could laugh out loud or say something funny, sly, or bold, then we won't see humor in the Gospel stories.

The humor of Jesus is not stand-up or sitcom; it takes several other forms. For our reading adventures, I've divided the texts into five categories: funny encounters, funny characters, funny images, funny miracles, all using texts from the Synoptic Gospels. The fifth category, humor in John, tries to undermine the notion that John is "the humorless Gospel." Each of these reading categories will also have a brief introduction.

I have included lots of examples, but not all that I've seen or others have suggested. No doubt you'll come to see humor on your own. Where the same example appears in more than one Gospel, I've listed the parallels but placed the one with the most promise or detail first.

Jesus' Funny Encounters

The title of Art Linkletter's old TV show, "People Are Funny," gives ample warning. If you hang out with people, as Jesus did, it's likely that someone will say something odd or act awkwardly, or even intentionally put you in a clumsy situation. The Gospels include stories of such moments.

Besides his disciples, the legal experts ("scribes") and Pharisees followed Jesus around, hoping to gather evidence they could use to discredit him, even kill him. The "gotcha" stories, featuring these religious leaders, are often fun. They used trick questions, trying to trap Jesus. Apparently they didn't know the story of the frustrated student who one day asked his teacher, "Rabbi, why do you always answer a question with a question?" The rabbi replied, "Why should I not answer a question with a question?" Rabbi Jesus knew this method and used it to reverse the trap on these hit squads. They would slink away to try again another day.

You might be amused at simple scenes like seeing folks trying to hush a blind man who is yelling for Jesus from the back edges of the crowd. One of my friends thinks it's funny that just after Jesus heals Peter's mother-in-law, she hops right up and fixes them lunch (Mark 1:29–31). Not that Jesus wouldn't have healed her anyway.

Matthew 21:23–27. An answer trap

The question team here has real clout—the chief priests and the elders. High-stakes "gotcha" game.

Matthew 22:15–22. Coin of the realm

To hear them talk, these folks must have been fans! But Jesus cuts through all that to ask who has a coin. Doug Adams points out that truly pious Jews wouldn't carry Caesar's coin. (He also notes, with a bit of created humor, that the story doesn't say that Jesus gave the coin back.)

Luke 7:31–35. A demon and a drunk

D****d if you do, d****d if you don't. Jesus challenges the no-win predicament.

Luke 7:36–50. Embarrassment to spare

Surprise, embarrassment, unexpected turns. I would guess there was awkward laughter in the moment and roars of laughter later.

Luke 14:7–11. The best seats in the house

Observing the clamor for seats and probably remembering old proverbs (see Proverbs 25:6–7), Jesus has fun with a story. Imagine yourself being there and taking it all in. Who's blushing? Who's mad? Who's grinning or laughing?

Luke 19:1–10. Scramble up, hurry down

Had he known, the short, rich guy might have hummed Randy Newman's "Short People" while he shinnied up the tree. But above all, he "was trying to see who Jesus was" (CEB). You could act out the story; I think it would be fun if André the Giant got the starring role. Enjoy people's reactions and dumbfounded looks throughout the story. Zacchaeus has surprises of his own.

Jesus' Funny Characters

Jesus used funny characters in his stories. Actually, we should better call them caricatures, since they are bigger-than-life, exaggerated images of people we know, or, if we can stand to be honest, of ourselves. You might even be tempted to name some of these characters after people you know. Or you might just give them nicknames based on their fatal flaws. The stories themselves are often funny, but the characters are a treat on their own. Small wonder that people loved listening to Jesus.

Luke 10:25–37. The no-good anti-hero

Perhaps you, like I, have heard lots of playful retellings of this shocking story. It has at least two threads of fun. The first is another "gotcha" thread where a smart Jewish lawyer tries to trap Jesus. In his questions and his story, Jesus eludes the trap and turns it back on the legal trickster, twice ending with "now go do that."

The second might have caught listeners off guard so much that they were too shocked to laugh, at first. Everything is upside-down except for the fact that you could get mugged and left for dead on the road from Jerusalem to Jericho. That was normal. According to Jewish teaching, which the lawyer had inquired about, the two who gave the victim a wide berth should have helped. And the one who did help is not someone you would ever call good, but one of those good-for-nothing, despised enemy, heretical Samaritans. Go figure. And "go do that."

Luke 11:5–8. Knocking at midnight

Jesus invites listeners into the story, "Suppose you go . . . and keep knocking." Suppose you do. Do you blush? Do you laugh? Or what? Is this normal? And don't forget "so what?"

Matthew 18:23–35. Debts huge and puny

When Jesus tells this story, Peter is probably still muttering, "And now I gotta forgive *and* do the math" (18:21–22). The fun of the high exaggerations and sudden turns in the story make it both convicting and memorable (even if you can't do the math).

Luke 14:16–24. Please excuse me. I, uh, . . .

When the servants told the invited guests that the great banquet was ready, they all (!) began to make excuses, lame excuses with fake urgency. The story includes only three examples, and the brief words of the third leave plenty of room for listeners to finish its humor. (Maybe you could imagine still other lame excuses they might have given.)

Note the host's movement from outrage to reckless generosity and the contrast between those who begged off and those the servants compelled to come.

Luke 16:1–9. The crooked manager

Parables, by design, puzzle you, rattle your cage, and leave you scratching your head. The one succeeds better than most. Funny lines and unexpected turns stir up laughter, too.

Luke 18:1–8. Nagging a corrupt judge

This story of two cartoonish characters and how they treat each other surely got a laugh—and made a point that sticks. Which of the two is most outrageous—the widow or the judge? How does the humor help strengthen Jesus' teaching here?

Luke 18:9–14. Thank you, God, that I'm so fine

These two characters beg to have their words read aloud with high exaggeration and passion. Flat affect or sweet and gentle reading neither gets the laugh nor nails the point.

Jesus' Funny Images

The best humorists get to funny fast; they keep comedy compact. Jesus mastered this, too. He delivered funny lines that were short, vivid, and memorable. They still pack a punch and stick with you. Most of the examples below use this quick-hit humor. You don't see them coming, but once you've seen them, you can't shake them. For many Bible readers, these sayings probably won't have the surprise power that strikes first-time hearers, but the images still have staying power. You'll enjoy them most if you don't blast past the visuals.

Matthew 5:29-30 (Matthew 18:8-9; Mark 9:43-47). Going to extremities

Missing the hyperbole and humor here can have dire consequences. Emergency room staff have seen literally far too many victims. Great laugh and strong message.

Matthew 7:3-4 (Luke 6:41-42). About that speck

You don't need a lot of coaching here. If you don't have a log in your eye, visualize it. Act it out. Sure, logs are huge. A cane or a chunk of firewood will do.

Matthew 19:23-24 (Mark 10:25; Luke 18:24-25). Cameling a needle

Yes, an ordinary needle.

Matthew 23:24. Sweating the small stuff

To follow a kosher diet, you have to pay attention to even small things, like gnats. For devout Jews, unclean foods included both gnats and camels. (So no camelized onions, etc.)

Matthew 7:9–11 (Luke 11:11–13). As bad as you are

The striking absurdity of the images lingers after the laughter. And before he gets to the point, Jesus teases parents a bit, knowing they often fear they're doing a lousy job.

Matthew 15:14 (Luke 6:39–40). Into a ditch

If you have trouble here, ask a friend who can help you see the point. Choose well.

Luke 11:24–26 (Matthew 12:43–45). Nice remodel! Thanks!

When, as a last resort, you return "home," it's nice to find it better than ever, clean and spiffy, ready for a party.

Mark 4:21–22 (Matthew 5:14–16; Luke 8:16). Hiding the light

"Hey, it's still kinda dark in here. I thought you brought a light."

Luke 17:37 (Matthew 24:28). Follow the vultures

The disciples want to know where to look "when that Day comes."

Matthew 23:1–12. Religion on parade

In high school I thought I was encouraged to carry my red Bible on top of my textbooks so people would know I really loved God. No doubt people had other ways of measuring. So, Jesus warns, watch out for the top-line religious folk who gear up to get noticed, with oversized prayer bands, reserved seats, and special titles.

Jesus' Funny Miracles

Miracles are amazing occasions, full of joy, tears, astonishment, and laughter. Awe and wonder overwhelm people, and they glorify God. Miracles can be funny, too. How it happens might amuse us. The circumstances, the when and where, can make us laugh. The delicious awkwardness of Jesus healing on the Sabbath, often, surely cracked up his disciples. After a while, they would see it coming. And sometimes the unexpected outcomes include grumps who are mad about the healing and the healed. "Who did this to you?!" The examples below include miracles that you might find funny.

Luke 5:1–11. If you say so . . .

The Gospels include some great fish stories, which seems right since Jesus' first disciples earned their livings as fishermen. Their hard work and experience set up this funny story.

Matthew 17:24–27. Tax fish

I pay a tax to fish; Peter fished to pay a tax. Do you think that by now Peter saw Jesus' instructions as normal? Of course, he's humored Jesus before.

Mark 2:1–12 (Matthew 9:1–8; Luke 5:17–26). The let-down

Season this crowded, dramatic scene with the four men frantically trying to get their friend to Jesus and with what the religious eagle-eyes' muttering stirs up.

Luke 8:26-39 (Matthew 8:28-34; Mark 5:1-20). Pigs possessed

Jesus is hardly out of the boat when a desperate man accosts him. Reading patiently and trying to see the details of the scene may lead from chuckles to "that's not really funny" to laughing out loud. (It's hard to ignore the pigs.) Note the interplay of awe and fear.

Mark 6:30-44 (Matthew 14:13-21; Luke 9:10-17; also in John). Lunch for 5,000

Jesus and his inner circle set out to find an isolated place, but the crowds beat them to it. That creates a food problem. We can enjoy Jesus' first solution to the problem more than the disciples did. The amount of money they mention was "worth almost eight months' pay" (CEB).

Matthew 14:22-33 (Mark 6:45-52). Water-walking

Enter in enough to feel the fear and hear the screaming. And, really, how could you not enjoy telling the story of Peter, the bold water-walker and sinking rock, for generations to come?

Luke 13:10-17. Straightening bent double

Stories of healing on the Sabbath often make me laugh, but this is one of the best. When Jesus called the woman to come to where he was teaching, it must have taken courage and hard effort for her to leave her women's separated place and come to this out-of-place. Her shouts of joy and praise, the grumpy synagogue leader, and the enthusiastic crowd create a funny scene.

Luke 8:40-42, 49-54 (Matthew 9:18-19; Mark 5:21-24, 35-43). The last laugh

Reading the three versions of this story makes it fuller. Perhaps the irony of the synagogue leader on his knees begging for his daughter's life is more tragic than funny. But it is funny how Jesus responded after folks said, "Don't bother," and when Jesus saw a crowd of mourners gathered at Jairus' home. He even got a laugh, or better, laughed at. I suspect that while the girl's parents were overcome with joy, Jesus got the last laugh.

Luke 8:42–48 (Matthew 9:20–22; Mark 5:25–34). Who touched me?

When you see the crowds, perhaps you can join with Peter in saying, "Well, that's a silly question!" The story unfolds from desperation to joy.

Humor in the Gospel of John

In the book I was reading the author was doing great identifying humor in the Bible—in Genesis, Judges, Esther, Jonah, in Jesus' life and teaching, in Acts, and more—when he made a sourpuss call that stopped me in my tracks. He called the Gospel of John "the humorless gospel." He said that it is "a definitively unlikely source" for humor and that it had a "dedicated anti-humor crusade," even though "there's humor everywhere else in the New Testament." How odd, I thought! "Good news (gospel)" and "anti-humor" don't go together at all. And the humor rises out of the joyful person Jesus was. So I started looking more closely.

Unlike the other Gospels, John doesn't include Jesus telling stories with odd characters or using quick-hit funny images (though using "born again" sure caught Nicodemus off guard). But stories about Jesus healing and responding to people include humor. The several examples below illustrate this, and we haven't included still others—the wisecracks that started the first meeting between Nathanael and Jesus (John 1), Jesus spooking his disciples by walking up to them on the Sea of Galilee (John 6), the tender and funny scene of Jesus trying to wash balky Peter's feet (John 13), and others.

John 2:1–11. Best 'til last

The story of the first of Jesus' miraculous signs spills over with humor. Linger a bit over his "Now, Mother!" responses to Mary. Enjoy and do the math on the six purification-rite jars at 20–30 gallons apiece ("two to three firkins" if you're still in King James).

And note the comments about saving the best wine until after the revelers can't tell the difference.

John 4:4–42. Where's your bucket?

The awkwardness in the story heightens its teaching and humor. Often Jews would avoid traveling through Samaria altogether and, as Eugene Peterson translates, "Jews in those days wouldn't be caught dead talking to Samaritans" (John 4:9, *The Message*). Here you have Jesus one-on-one, mid-day at Jacob's Well.

Try to view the conversation through the tool "Imagine them smiling." What if you see this as banter? It leads to more substance, of course. Wonder, too, how the woman would respond to Jesus recounting her personal history. This surprise amuses readers, of course. Look for other surprise, doesn't-fit, and reversal elements.

John 5:1–18. Do you want to get well?

Another healing-on-the-Sabbath story, typically with fun edges in both healing and conflict. The in-your-face response in John 5:17 didn't amuse the Jewish leaders, but it might make readers smile.

John 6:1–15. Can't even afford snacks

In this telling of the story, Jesus initiates the conversation about feeding the crowd. Many translations say that Jesus "tested" Philip, though you might see "tease" in it, too, a bit of playfulness. As you reflect on the whole story, you might also imagine that you are Philip.

John 8:2–11. Where's that first stone?

Jesus again slips through the "gotcha" trap the religious leaders set. The humor comes in how adeptly Jesus escapes their question and embarrasses them all at once. Try to see the leaders bursting in on Jesus already teaching, the silences as Jesus writes in the dirt, and the awkwardness as the accusers slink away, oldest to youngest. And it ends with Jesus' compassion, by this time no surprise, no joke.

John 9:1–41. Now I see

This extended humorous story can be broken into six episodes, each with distinct characters and movement in the storyline. The funny dialogues explore the questions of healing on the Sabbath and of who Jesus really is. Try reading the dialogues aloud, letting your voice(s) reflect the excitement, curiosity, fear, and cheekiness. Follow the I-don't-knows.

John 11:38–46. That awful smell

Of course it would be Martha, the sister of good order, who objects, "But, Lord . . . ." Do you think some folks would have laughed as they saw Lazarus try to emerge from the tomb-cave bound hand and foot? Or that he came out at all? Why else?

John 21:1–14. Catch of the day!

Another fish story, and a great one to walk through in your imagination. These guys prove they're fishermen, too, by keeping track of how big and how many (153!). Perhaps they were "St. Peter's Fish," medium-sized bass in the Sea of Galilee.

Humor in Acts

The emerging church described in the book of Acts was a vital community, full of energy and joy. Luke, a doctor who accompanied Paul on some of his missionary travels is probably the author of this book as well as the Gospel of Luke, which Acts continues. Lots of fun things happened in the life of the church and the early Christians surely loved telling these stories laced with wonder, humor, rejoicing, and more. Dr. Luke shows he had a great sense of humor and no doubt he and Paul often swapped funny memories and stories as they travelled. Maybe you can see in the passages below some of the stories they told over and over again with great delight. Again, look for the devices of humor that we've come to expect: surprise, exaggeration, absurdity, irony, reversals, etc. These passages suggest several possibilities to explore whether and where you think they used humor.

Acts 3:1–11; 4:5–22. Stumped by a leaper

This leaping fellow had sat at the temple gate, unable to walk, probably for decades. Lots of people recognized him and maybe even had given him money. But for the temple personnel, praising God for the man's healing was not the first thing that came to mind.

Acts 5:17–26. So where'd they go?

Where Peter and John started is the last place the leaders looked.

The following pair of stories describes how God confounds Peter as an observant Jew. Being devout required him to avoid hanging out with pagan (non-Jewish) folk and to eat only kosher foods. Peter tells this story again in Acts 11:1–18, explaining how this affected him. It's not an easy change. Paul writes about how he had to call Peter out for eating only with Jews after bigwigs from Jerusalem showed up in Antioch (Galatians 2:11–14).

Acts 10:1–8, 17–33. Visiting Cornelius, the not-so-pagan Roman centurion

Notice how this unexpected invitation comes about and follow what happens once Peter shows up.

Acts 10: 9–17. The non-kosher buffet

And Peter was hungry, just praying a bit before having a good lunch.

Acts 12:1–19. Peter sprung from prison. Really?

Both episodes here—the escape and the prayer meeting—offer fun details to see as you read.

Acts 14:8–20. Hard to stay human

Since Paul was doing the talking, he became the Greek god Hermes, the messenger god, while Barnabas suddenly was Zeus, the chief of the Greek pantheon, father of the gods, and ruler of the heavens. They probably had not written this on that day's to-do list.

Acts 16:25–39. Suicidal jailer and horrified officials

The singing may have been alarming enough, but the earthquake really turned things upside-down.

Acts 19:11–20. Jewish exorcists take a beating

Obviously there's good money in exorcism and great value in adding to your bag of tricks. What would make you burn your bag of tricks?

Acts 20:7-12. The risks of sleeping through a sermon

"The Fall," for Eutychus, was more than a theological term. Notice what Paul does after he reassures everyone that the guy lying on the ground is fine, not dead.

Acts 21:37-40; 22:22-29. Paul rescued from a riot

These episodes happen near the Antonia Fortress, a Roman police station at the northwest corner of the temple area. Part of the fun here is to see how Paul works the Roman soldiers as they are rescuing him and beginning to interrogate him.

Acts 23:6-10 (context: Acts 22:30—23:5). Paul stirs up the Sanhedrin

Do you think Paul's tactic here would work every time? There's nothing quite like throwing out such juicy theological bait!

Acts 24-26. Paul on trial

This series of courtroom scenes offers a tangled web of flattering speech, earnest witness, confusion, indecision, and passing the buck—all in all, quite a jolly jumble.

Acts 27. Throwing and going overboard

Mr. If-only-you-had-listened-to-me directs sailors, soldiers, and all 276 folks on board to safety.

Acts 28:1-6. Snake-bit

From murderer to god!

Humor in Paul

In his letters, the apostle Paul reveals a robust sense of humor. Sometimes it's subtle and sometimes it's broad and bold. He teases to teach, uses grand exaggeration, enjoys parody and reversal, and even creates vivid comic pictures. We have great examples, but Paul's humor doesn't show up everywhere.

Smart humorists know their audiences and adapt to their needs. I suspect that's why most of our examples are from Paul's letters to Christians at Corinth. Paul had founded that church, and he and the believers gathered there knew each other well. They all knew how they could kid and laugh and joke with each other. Compare, on the other hand, the letter to people in Rome. Paul writes to them before he has met most of them and he apparently keeps his humor in check. Again, in contrast, Paul doesn't hold back with his friend Philemon as he "humors" him to be kind to Onesimus.

If you want to explore more, Douglas Adams has an engaging chapter on Paul's humor in his book *The Prostitute in the Family Tree*. He adds examples to the ones we've chosen here.

1 Corinthians 1:10–17. Foggy memory

Paul fondly calls these believers "my loved children" (4:14). They have come from all segments of society into unity in Christ. Except now various groups pose as better than others based on the teacher they admire, who baptized them, or what spiritual gifts they have. Throughout the letter Paul has to address this party spirit. He speaks directly, but he sneaks in some teasing, even feigning forgetfulness, to undercut the brags of baptism.

1 Corinthians 1:18–31. Bragging rights

After wonderful teaching about foolishness and weakness, Paul needs an example. So in verse 26 and following he teases and pushes back on the braggadocio problem: "Well, look at yourselves."

1 Corinthians 4:6–13. Fools for Christ

Paul uses a lot of upside-down images and teasing here. Try reading Paul's troubles with an "I-don't-get-no-respect" tone of voice. It's not bragging.

1 Corinthians 7:1–11, 18. Self-control and other matters

Adams points out that Paul has delayed answering some of the Corinthians' questions up to this point, so "Now, about what you wrote." He also toys a bit by giving both/and answers to what they presented as either/or questions. As the Corinthians heard Paul's counsel as sex advisor read out, can you imagine with me some nudges and chuckles in the group. Oh yes, and don't try to fix that (v. 18).

1 Corinthians 12. What a big eye you have!

Paul also uses the metaphor of the church as the Body of Christ in Romans 12 and Ephesians 4, but only here does he launch into such a humorous riff. Go with it! Visualize the word pictures. Read the dissenting voices out loud. The pride-of-place arguing gets taken down in laughter.

1 Corinthians 13:1–7. Gong show

Imagine a clash of voices with various folk loudly bragging up their gifts—tongues, prophecy, great faith, charitable giving, etc. And then against that noise hear gentle words like these: "Love is not envious or boastful or arrogant or rude . . . ." Can you see silly here?

2 Corinthians 11:1—12:13. Put up with a fool

The humor cues here should put us on alert. Paul says he's speaking like a "fool." He uses sarcasm with the label "super-apostles." And he gives an upside-down list of his credentials. Adams calls this approach an "antiautobiography." The Greeks and Romans often used self-flattering autobiographies, an ancient practice that endures, especially in election years. Notice how sharply Paul's claims differ from bragging about being in *Who's Who*; being the Man of the Year; being welcomed by presidents, kings, and CEOs; Chairman of the Board; chosen for the Genius Award, etc. Paul has been on a board alright, but not that kind of board. In this resume he is "bragging about [his] weaknesses" (11:30). Though this is a letter, I find it helpful to try to speak out his words with pauses and inflection appropriate to "speaking like a crazy person" (11:23).

Galatians 5:1–12. Cutting humor

This letter shows clearly that Paul has had it with the folks who were teaching the Galatians that men still needed to be circumcised to become followers of Christ. In verse 12 his disgust gives way to some circumcision humor. Translations vary, though the sense is clear. My favorite translation, though it is a bit too polite, is still from *The Jerusalem Bible*: "Tell those who are disturbing you I would like to see the knife slip."

Philippians 3:4–8. Just a pile of skybalon

Here again Paul gives a humorous mistreatment of his fine pedigree by using the climactic and scatological Greek word *skybalon*. I didn't know that Greek word when I first laughed at this, but the old translation "dung" was fun, and less polite words were accurate and even more fun. I notice that the fine *Common English Bible*, which is meant to be read aloud in church, sticks with the family-friendly "sewer trash."

Philemon. Persuading with humor

Perhaps you've been played by a good friend who wants you to do something hard and uses arm-twisting and gentle joking to get you to do it. Your friend "humors" you. Paul's letter to Philemon is an exquisite example of such humoring.

Paul's request is stunning. He asks Philemon to welcome back his runaway slave Onesimus, to treat him well, and even to treat him "as a dearly loved brother" (v. 16). By law, Philemon could treat him harshly and even execute him, which is also harsh.

Paul uses praise and flattery that is both sincere and a bit overdone, the kind of praise that makes you wonder, "So what does he want?" He plays authority against love, toys with who owes who, reminds Philemon that he, Paul, is an old man in prison for the gospel, and then, with a wide smile, adds that he knows Philemon will do more than he asks. To the full, loving arm-twist he adds, "And get a room ready for me."

Soak in the radical request and in how cleverly Paul weaves humor into his asking. Perhaps you could imagine being Philemon.

III.

Reports from the Field

I'M AN EXPLORER MYSELF, of course. I've gladly added looking for humor to all the other tools and ways of reading that I use to understand the Bible. I'm sure that I still have a lot to learn.

The essays in this section grow out of my explorations. Many of them come directly from reading and responding to biblical texts. In others, the texts interact with authors and ideas. All of them share my discoveries.

The Unhidden Revealed

The looks on their faces stick with me still. Long-time friends Kenneth and Edna had asked about my study of humor in the Bible and listened politely as I eagerly told them about the humor in the story of Abraham and Sarah being told they'll have a baby. But my friends didn't get it. Devout and creative, each with a great sense of humor, they didn't get it. Puzzled, I tried a different approach. I asked how they would react, now that they were in their mid-80s, if a messenger from God would tell them they were going to have a baby. Long pause. Light in his eyes and a hearty chuckle; light in her eyes, too, a smaller chuckle, and a fleeting look that bordered on terror. That look has since helped me ponder Sarah.

In talking about humor in the Bible, I often start with the story of geriatric Abraham and Sarah because it, quite literally, has laughter written all over it. Abraham laughs, Sarah laughs, everybody else laughs, they name the baby Laughter, or He-Laughs (Isaac). But, as obvious as it is, many readers don't get it because they don't expect to find humor in the Bible at all. Or, more sharply, in taking the Bible seriously, they reject the idea that it might include humor.

I've avoided market-savvy titles like "The Bible's Hidden Humor Revealed," mostly because humor in the Bible is not hidden. It's all over the place. It's in the Old Testament stories, in Proverbs, in the Prophets, in Jesus' teaching, in Acts, in Paul, and more. We just need to expect it and learn to see it.

Reading the Bible well requires that we pay careful attention not only to what the writers say, but also to how they say it. It requires that we stay open to what's there, including to the possibility that writers might use humor as a powerful tool to say important things.

God, That's Funny

My friend Dan helped me even more than he knew. Not that he wouldn't have done it anyway. He sent me links to essays on humor from an unlikely source, one he knew I wouldn't see. And they were pretty good, except for one by Joel Kilpatrick that I suspect a careless editor let by. It was terrific. Kilpatrick is the brains behind larknews.com, a satirical (Onion-like) Christian site where you can find headlines like "Family buys hut next to sponsored child" or "Pastor welcomes birth of second sermon illustration" or a news article about a church stuck with a worship leader who specializes in "alien folk music." So I laughed and learned that larknews.com is still around (cheers!) and that Kilpatrick has written a fun and insightful book, *GOD, That's Funny*.

The book will startle some readers, I'm sure, because Kilpatrick combines humor with God and considers this combo to be foundational, not simply frivolous or decorative. "We all need to be reminded that God is funny," he writes, "[t]hat his humor is on display everywhere and is a key to understanding what he's doing in our lives, in Scripture, and in the world around us. We all need to appreciate that comedy is one of God's primary languages." He challenges even more pointedly about our relationship with God: "God has never been without humor, and if we live in his presence, neither can we."

Always funny and often poignant, Kilpatrick develops this theme out of his personal experience, his well-honed humor skills, and his reading of the Bible. He shows humor in the Bible in Old Testament stories like geriatric Abraham and Sarah having a baby, but also uses unexpected Old Testament texts. He stirs readers' imaginations and insight when he analyzes the steps of humor in Jesus' teaching, healing, and conversations with folks. (I especially enjoyed his take on the story of Jesus chatting with the woman at the well in Samaria.) In my case, at least, he stretched and deepened my understanding of the absurdity and upside-down character of Jesus' "incarnation," which he describes as "pure hilarity to me, the strongest possible satire of human power and pretense."

Kilpatrick calls readers to a new dimension in their life with God: "This is the pattern of God, to provoke surprise and laughter, and then to invite us into an astonished, sincere, loving relationship with him that looks nothing like we expected." Maybe it's time here for a show of hands, even an altar call. Hum along, joyfully. If you can't do that, you can at least read the book.

Funny and Ugly

Sometimes funny and ugly can show up all at once. In this instance, I don't mean in people, but in a story. I remembered this while my pastor was preaching a very good sermon on Genesis 38, the story of Judah and Tamar. (Who preaches on Judah and Tamar?! This is the first I've heard.) The sermon rightly described Judah's irresponsible and demeaning behavior toward his widowed daughter-in-law Tamar, and doing that even before she tricked him into using her services when she disguised herself as a prostitute. Rather than following Judah's ugly example, our pastor insisted, we should treat everyone, women and men, with dignity and respect, as whole persons, a particularly challenging path in our highly sexualized society.

I got the point, but I also laughed (not out loud). The text uses two funny pieces to drive home, not distract from, its message. The first is the story of Judah making arrangements to hire Tamar as a hooker. He promises to pay her a goat, but she demands something to secure his pledge. In this instance, she requests and Judah gives her his seal and cord (a personalized seal used to sign contracts written on clay) and his staff. In effect, Judah gives her his credit card and other evidence that will clearly identify him. Trying to deal with this discreetly, Judah later sends a goat with a friend to pay her and to retrieve his pledge. The friend's search shows subtle humor. In recounting how Judah hired Tamar, Genesis 38:15 refers to her with the Hebrew word for an ordinary prostitute. When the friend searches for her and tries to pay her, however, he uses the Hebrew word for "shrine prostitute" or "holy prostitute." Many modern translations capture this change.

Judah is trying to save face here, to make his dalliance a bit more respectable (even though Israelites knew that using "shrine prostitutes" was not acceptable practice). When the locals respond that they don't remember seeing a "shrine prostitute" around there, Judah decides not to keep trying to recover his credit card, lest he "become a laughingstock." So storytellers and listeners will laugh at Judah trying to escape being laughed at.

The seal and staff show up again in a story that explodes with surprise and reversal, a story that gets a laugh. Not from Judah, but from everyone else. When Judah is told that Tamar has played the prostitute and is now three months pregnant, he flies into a (self-)righteous rage. "Bring her out and have her burned to death!" he orders. The story continues: "As she was being brought out, she sent a message to her father-in-law. 'I am pregnant by the man who owns these,' she said. And she added, 'See if you recognize whose seal and cord and staff these are'" (Genesis 38:25, NIV).

He recognized them; so did everyone around him. Now maybe you don't laugh when a guy in a righteous rage gets caught with his pants down, so to speak. But a lot of us do. Laughing here doesn't lighten Judah's offense but, instead, puts the exclamation point on his treachery. Now Judah is laughingstock; Judah gets nailed.

He could hardly escape the truth of Tamar having his American Express card, but in some measure (half-hearted, in my opinion), he owns up to his failure. Traditional translations read here, "She is more righteous than I," which doesn't really award anyone a blue ribbon for "righteousness." The sense is that in the history of their long relationship, Tamar had acted more responsibly than Judah. *The Message* captures it, "She's in the right; I'm in the wrong . . . ."

So funny and ugly sometimes go together, not news to those who watch Jon Stewart take on tough issues on *The Daily Show*. We can use laughter both to entertain and to make a point. We shouldn't be surprised that the Bible does that, too.

A postscript, also with a funny twist: Tamar bore Judah twin boys. The first was named Perez, and according to Matthew 1:3, he was one of the not-quite-kosher ancestors of Jesus.

The Voila! Moment

Sometimes funny bits pop up suddenly in the midst of clamor and tumult, when the scene is dark and ominous. So we laugh and catch our breath at the comic relief while drama quickly overtakes us again. That happens in high-tension "action" movies and in horror films (so I'm told; I'm not a fan). It also happens in Exodus.

Starting in Exodus 19, the Bible describes Israel at Sinai, sometimes shaking as the mountain was quaking, covered with cloud and fire, a brilliant light they associated with the presence or the glory of God. Overwhelmed Israel pleaded with Moses that he should tell them what God says, but not let God speak to them directly.

In that context Israel agreed to making a covenant with Yhwh (the "Lord"), had received the Ten Commandments, had engaged in dramatic covenant-ratification ceremonies, and had heard the "covenant scroll" read out with all of the Lord's words, case law, and more. Right after that God calls Moses and Joshua, his assistant, on into the cloud and higher up the mountain, and they go.

After a good, long while (actually about seven weeks), the people complain to Aaron, leader pro-tem, also Moses' brother, "prophet" for Moses, and companion in confronting Pharaoh. "Make us gods who can lead us. Moses has been gone a long time and we have no idea about what has happened to him." Aaron complied, collecting gold, using a tool to shape the image of a bull calf, and setting up a festival to worship and celebrate, ironically a festival for Yhwh! (Exodus 32:1–6)

God notices and is infuriated by this breach of the brand-new covenant, so angry, in fact, that God tells Moses (still in the cloud) that God will ditch Israel, "your people whom you brought out of Egypt," and start over with Moses. I'm amused that Moses talks God out of it: Israel was *your*, not my, idea; this is "your own people whom you brought out of Egypt"; you've made promises going way back; you'll make yourself look bad in the Egyptian press (Exodus 32:7–14).

When Moses and Joshua came down from the mountain, carrying the stone tablets covered front and back with God's own writing, the worship party was even more out of control than God had warned. Moses shattered the tablets, destroyed the idol, punished the people, and then turned to Aaron, "What did these people do to you . . . ?"—an opening for Aaron's entry for stupid answer of the year.

"Don't be so mad, sir. Calm down. You yourself know how rotten these people can be. They demanded, 'Make us gods to lead us since we have no idea about what happened to Moses.' (What were you thinking?) So I collected their gold, threw it into the fire, and—*voila!*—out came this bull calf." Ka-boom! (Exodus 32:22–24).

The voila! moment gets me every time. No, Aaron didn't speak French, I know, and voila! would look ugly written in Hebrew. Maybe you would prefer, "Behold . . . (drum roll) . . . a burnished bull." Or, "Who would have guessed?!" What surprise! What innocence! Do you think Aaron blushed? Of course he didn't fool Moses, who knew that Aaron had let, no, actually helped, the people get out of control.

Is Aaron's answer normal? Well, yes, it is. We humans like to make excuses, avoid blame, and distance ourselves from the scene, even when we're caught pants-down and red-handed. It's usually lame and sad and funny.

Donkey-Speak

The Old Testament story about a talking donkey cracks me up. But I have to choose how to speak accurately and politely about this animal. Apparently this is a female (a "jenny") and also a true ass (Equus asinus), the species that brays "hee-haw," not a half-ass (Equus hemionus). "Ass" has had a respectable history, winding its way through Greek, Old Norse, Old High German, Old English, and Middle English down to the present day. The translators of the Jewish Publication Society use the word "ass" in the story, and these people know a thing or two. But most of the rest of the English translators use "donkey" or even "she-donkey." Maybe this is courtesy to tender ears.

So mostly I'll use polite donkey-speak in talking about Balaam's "donkey." This is one of two related funny stories buried in what seems an unlikely place, the book of Numbers. Numbers is a mishmash of lists of names, clans, numbers (!); laws about life and ritual practice; stories of traveling in the wilderness; and a bit of debauchery. But chapters 22–24 throw in high humor full of surprise and reversal.

The first story frames the second. King Balak of Moab was scared of the Israelites, who were then perched at his borders, and wanted to hire a reputable religious guru to curse them. So he sent for Balaam with a lucrative offer and high confidence: "For this I know: whomever you bless is blessed, whomever you curse is cursed" (22:6). The story is a little fuzzy on whether it's okay for Balaam to do this, but eventually he agrees to do it with the caveat that he can only say what God allows him to say. Three times, on three different overlooks, the Moabites build seven altars and on each of them sacrifice bulls and rams. And three times Balaam blesses Israel at the expense of Moab. After the first occasion, King Balak protests, "What have you done to me? I brought you to curse my enemies, and you heap blessings on them!" (23:11). But he hires Balaam twice more! After the third time, "Balak flew into a rage with Balaam. He beat his hands together and said to Balaam, 'I brought you to curse my enemies, and you bless them three times over!" Balaam is all innocence, reminding the king that he had warned that he could only say what God told him. The piling up of extravagance, reversal, and failure in face of the king's desperation is funny storytelling.

The talking ass donkey is even better. The story is wonderfully told, and I invite you to read it with your imagination open for business. (See Numbers 22:22–35.) Be clear, of course, that this is not Mr. Ed, the talking horse of ancient TV fame, or the sassy donkey of the movies Shrek. The donkey here has served Balaam well for a long time with never more than a true ass "hee-haw." It is on this reliable beast that Balaam sets out on his questionable journey. As mostly a city kid, I don't know much personally about donkeys except for participating once in a donkey basketball game. They say donkeys can have a mind of their own, and it looks like that in this story. First, she goes running off the road into a field. Then she knocks her rider's foot against a vineyard's stone wall. Finally, she simply lies down under him. Each time Balaam beats her with a stick, the last time so furiously that he'd just as soon have killed her.

That's when the faithful donkey, with God's help, starts to talk. "What have I done to you? Why beat me three times like this?" Balaam storms on that she has made a fool of him and he'd kill her if he had a sword. The donkey continues, and here you have to choose a voice or tone to interpret the sense. Is it accusing, mournful, puzzled, indignant, or _____? I usually go with indignant sob story. Choose a voice, read it out loud, and put yourself into it. "Am I not your donkey, and have I not been your mount from youth? In all this time, have I ever failed to serve you?" (Come on, get some tears into it.) Balaam: "No."

Now, for the first time, Balaam sees the messenger/angel of Yhwh who has been standing in the road with a drawn sword. All this time, the donkey has been seeing what the seer ("the one with far-seeing eyes" [24:3]) can't see. The angel scolds Balaam for beating his donkey and then explains, "You're lucky she did turn aside, or I should have killed you by now—though I would have spared her!" (I laugh every time at this tag line.) Of course, by now Balaam, even more than the donkey, is all ears. He repents and promises to do whatever he's told, which sets up the stories of King Balak's sacrifices and saying only what God tells him to say.

Here humor serves the writer's larger themes well, and it invites us to enjoy it when it shows up. We don't need to be too earnest here in squeezing out hidden meanings. A seminarian once offered me this application: "If God could speak through Balaam's ass, then God can speak through yours." But I don't think we need to go there. Just let the texts live, breathe, and giggle.

Mayhem, Shenanigans, and Hanky-Panky

In evaluating a Bible survey course, one student objected that the course included too much sex and violence. I don't think that was only in the session I guest-taught. They must have actually read the Bible and been surprised at how much sex and violence is there. The title *Holy Bible* doesn't entice readers by promising juicy stuff like adultery, murder, love songs, war, and mayhem. Maybe that would be "The Shocking-Truths-Revealed-and-Illustrated Bible." (In a reversal of not promising, I discovered years ago that Augustine's *Confessions*, unlike a magazine of the same name, hardly included any racy stuff at all.) Advertised or not, though, the stories of the Bible mix in more mayhem, shenanigans, and hanky-panky than you would expect.

The stories of Samson, the "judge," have plenty of all three (see Judges 13–16). God used Samson to rescue the Israelites from their neighbors, the Philistines, but hardly because he was the poster boy of true devotion. One persistent theme in the book of Judges is how God chooses and uses unlikely people to protect and lead Israel. The stories make clear, I think, that Samson tops the unlikely list.

The stories about Samson are also very entertaining. They are like many stories about folk heroes, and they are told with relish. Often using great humor, folk hero stories typically tell of the hero's prowess, cleverness, fatal flaws, near escapes, and final victories, all of which we have in Samson. He was born to unsuspecting country folk and was given secret powers (if he kept his hair—apparently male pattern baldness was not an issue). He could rip lions in half, carry the doors of Gaza's city gates uphill 35 miles overnight (a feat reminiscent of Paul Bunyan), and kill a thousand enemy warriors with the jawbone of an ass. (This last image, as I mentioned earlier, has been used to speak unflatteringly of annoying public speakers.) He could think up puzzling riddles, and with cleverness and prowess was able to capture 300 foxes, tie pairs of them together by their tails, set their tails on fire, and turn the foxes loose in his enemies' grain fields. These are mayhem and shenanigan stories, for sure.

For hanky-panky, we can go to the stories (yes, plural) about Samson's fatal flaw. He found the Philistine (!) women irresistible and was a sucker for fine form and fluttering eyelashes. The dialogues of Samson trying to respond to her "If you really loved me . . ." are priceless, sad, funny, and the stuff of thousands of plays and sitcoms since. We can still read them aloud with high humor without changing a word.

The Bible tells, sometimes playfully, the story of God's presence in real human life, including the parts that are embarrassing, ugly, and seamy. Often, for all our sake, we have to include humor to respond to and understand the glory and failure we share.

David's Daring Dowry

Saul wanted to kill David, though even for a king it's hard to knock off a war hero. Still he tried, throwing spears at him, dispatching hit squads, sending him off to war so the Philistines would do the dirty work, and marrying him to his daughters. Saul promised him his oldest daughter, Merab, but when David didn't get killed in battle, Saul gave her to someone else. Daughter Michal later fell in love with David and, after some roundabout negotiations, Saul offered a deal on the princess' dowry. You can read all about it in 1 Samuel 18:20–29 and see if you think it's as funny as I do.

Just a word of summary and background. Saul was willing to give his daughter to David, not for cash, but in exchange for one hundred Philistine foreskins. I think Saul and I would agree that war is one thing, but swiping a guy's foreskin is quite another. After all, it's not like picking pockets. It's up close and personal. He'll notice and probably won't volunteer. Verse 27 tells us that David and his men doubled the deal, collecting two hundred foreskins. David brought them to Saul and, as *The Jerusalem Bible* properly translates, "counted them out before the king." One, two, three . . .

Awful Funny

Just like comic scenes in horror movies (I'm not an expert on this), the Bible sometimes mixes funny stories into awful storylines. Jamming tragedy and comedy together shows vividly in the stories about Michal (mee-kahl), King Saul's youngest daughter.

Part of the tragedy is that both Saul and David used Michal for their own purposes. Saul used her to try to kill David. He had progressed from being insulted that David got more credit as a warrior than he did to fearing him, hating him, and eventually to making him a constant enemy. David, on the other hand, used Michal to become a legitimate part of the royal family. Before Samuel had anointed him, David hadn't much thought about being king, but he quickly warmed to the idea. He pursued it steadily with a dynamic blend of cunning, prowess, and blessing. (He wasn't entirely ruthless, since he carried some of foreign-woman Ruth's DNA.) Marrying Michal gave him an edge in becoming king.

Yet in the midst of all this chaos and conflict, Michal loved David. As did her brother Jonathan and everybody in Israel. Except Saul. Seeing that Michal loved David, Saul offered her to David as wife, requiring as a dowry only one hundred Philistine foreskins. David would get killed for sure, he thought, before he collected a bag full of those. But he didn't, and David took Michal as wife.

After Saul failed to get his family and servants to kill David, he took direct action, but the daughter he offered as bait thwarts him. (See 1 Samuel 19:8–18 for these stories.) First he sends a surveillance squad to stake out David's house to keep track of him. Michal knows trouble is brewing and warns David to flee that night. She sneakily lets him down from a window (an underserved biblical theme—see also spies at Jericho, Saul at Damascus, Eutychus at Troas), and David runs for his life. Then she puts a household idol in his bed, tops it with a goat-hair wig, and throws covers over it. Many of us may best remember this age-old trick from the movie *Ferris Bueller's Day Off*, but it's a perennial one.

The next morning, as Michal predicted, Saul sends a hit squad to murder David. Now here the biblical text is very compact, so we need to use our imaginations a bit to unpack the story, to see faithfully what the author describes.

When the hit squad arrives at David's house and they ask to see him, Michal greets them and says, "Sorry, he's sick today. You'll have to come another time." So the bewildered assassins leave and return to Saul, willing to put off murdering David until he was feeling better. That's funny in itself, but imagine what they had to tell Saul: "Umm, he's sick today so we couldn't kill him." Remember that this is the Saul who, when he's angry, throws spears at people. Might he have said, "I don't care if he's sick, I want him dead!"? Among other things, Saul ordered them back to David's house, "Bring him, bed and all, back so I can kill him!" (*The Message*).

They hurry back, barge into David's room, and find only the dummy with the goat-hair wig, but they bring Michal back to Saul. He challenges her, "How could you betray me, play tricks on me, and side with my enemy?!" Michal, ever resourceful, has one more trick, "David threatened me. He said, 'Help me get away or I'll kill you!'" She survives this crisis, though Saul gives her as wife to another man.

Michal's story continues, after Saul's death, in texts that also blend tragedy and humor, but for now let's note how trickery, surprise, and reversal can weave humor through ugly stories. And maybe you, with me, will continue to wonder whether the spirited Michal was naïve or ambitious or clever.

Covered with Glory

It wasn't the best day of Michal's life, though her husband David, starring in the huge ark-comes-to-Jerusalem parade, acted like it was one of his. She watched through a palace window, growing angrier by the minute. David was ecstatic, leaping, dancing, and giving it everything he had without even a thought about who was watching him prance around in his odd priestly gear. After all, he was bringing the revered ark of the covenant to Jerusalem, finally, with high hopes that it would bring blessing to him and the city, that it would please God, and that it would be a good political move, to boot.

The parade was bursting with extravagance—crowds shouting, trumpets sounding, sacrifices offered after every six steps of progress. Once the Ark was finally at rest in its sacred tent, David offered more sacrifices, he blessed the people in God's name, and he generously gave gifts to everyone who came. Michal, watching all of this, came to despise David ("in her heart"!) and could not restrain her contempt.

So when David came home to bless his own household, Michal went out to meet him. "You sure covered yourself with glory today, Mr. King," she started sarcastically, "leaping and dancing and showing off way too much of your royal anatomy so even the servant girls could stare at it, just like any vulgar guy would!" To David, this didn't sound like "Welcome home, dear. How was your day?"

Jamming a ferocious family fight smack-dab against such an amazing day is jarring, a mismatch, and in that way kind of funny. That tone continues with David.

David's sharp response wasn't much like the blessing he intended to give. First, a bit defensive, "I was dancing and leaping for the Lord, not for them." Then boom!—". . . the Lord who chose me, instead of your father and your family, to lead Israel." Oh, "And I'm going to celebrate even more, might even humiliate myself, but these servant girls will honor me." That's all, but plenty enough to get a headline "Row in Royal Family" in the ancient *National Enquirer*. It even made the Bible!

One more thing. The author notes that Michal never had children. Some commentators say God closed her womb, but the text doesn't say that. I would guess that the text suggests, instead, that closing her womb wasn't really necessary. Its brevity may simply be a wry "no further comment." (See 2 Samuel 6:12–23.)

Witty Wisdom

I love having a pro agree with me, so finding Garrison Keillor reflecting on his work and quoting Ecclesiastes made my day. "Comedy does give good value," he writes.

> There are so many discouraging facts around—e.g., half of all people are below average—and jokes relieve some of the misery. Solomon said, "Whoever increases knowledge increases sorrow." That's a joke. And "The rivers run into the sea and yet the sea is not full." That's a joke. And how about this one? "The race is not to the swift nor the battle to the strong nor riches to men of understanding, but time and chance happeneth to them all." That's the essence of comedy in less than 25 words.
> (In *AARP Bulletin*, May 2014. Yes, I've received this for years now.)

Jokes do relieve misery just as they often grow out of misery. Jokes spring out of surprises, odd reversals, funny tensions and contradictions, and quirkiness in life. Their humor helps us cope, but it can also teach and guide us. Using humor, the wisdom literature in the Bible teaches us but also helps make the teaching memorable. Effective humor helps ideas stick.

Proverbs in the Bible (and anywhere else) are supposed to stick in your head, not from rote memorization, but because they're witty, funny, short, full of word play, and spot-on true. Of course, they're not all funny, but many are. I've been enjoying a "Polish proverb" recently on how to resist being drawn into other people's conflicts: "Not my circus, not my monkeys." Biblical proverbs can have the same punch. How about, "The words of a fool start fights; do him a favor and gag him" (18:6, *The Message*). Or, "Even dunces who keep quiet are thought to be wise; as long as they keep their mouths shut, they're smart" (17:28). Maybe this: "The shopper says, 'That's junk—let me take it off your hands,' then goes off boasting of the bargain" (20:14). Unlike Keillor, I've used the modern language of Peterson's *The Message*, partly to help us see funny phrases in a language we actually use. But the larger point, of course, is that humor shows up in the Bible's wisdom literature. We should expect it, look for it, and welcome it.

I've chosen examples from Proverbs, Keillor from Ecclesiastes, and along the way I'll write about humor in Job. All three use humor to nail the truth. Here's a take-along: "Yes, there's a right time and way for everything, even though, unfortunately, we miss it for the most part" (Ecclesiastes 8:6). In comedy and in life, great timing is everything, but half of us are below average. You can choose your half.

Humor in Job?

When I tease at the possibility that the book of Job uses humor, some folks fire back, "How could Job be funny? It's such a tragic story!" It is, of course. But sometimes writers use humor in very dark places. Flannery O'Connor uses it in her short stories. The Bible uses it, too. Darkness covers the story of Jacob stealing Esau's blessing from Isaac, but the goatskins on Jacob's arms to help him pose as his hairy brother add comic relief. Wisdom literature from the ancient Near East, such as *The Dialogue of Pessimism*, which explores similar themes as Job, often uses humor. So I suggest that in Job, sometimes humor and tragedy mingle.

The story needs to show Job right away as the best person in the history of the cosmos. It starts abruptly: "Job was a man who lived in Uz. He was honest inside and out, a man of his word, who was totally devoted to God and hated evil with a passion" (Job 1:1, *The Message*). The author not only states the premise of the story, Job's integrity and devotion to God, but also exaggerates it, makes it bigger than life. This is caricature, an oversized way of making a point and making people smile.

Job loves God so much that he even tries to be devoted to God on behalf of his kids. Apparently his adult children, seven sons and three daughters, liked to party, feasting and boozing at each other's homes. And after every late night party, Job would get up in the early morning to offer top-of-the-line sacrifices for each of his children, worrying that, partied out, they might have "cursed God in their hearts." Job did this regularly. Most of us know this guy and shake our heads as we laugh and cry.

Between his impeccable integrity and his impressive wealth, Job was the best man in the whole territory. As God points out to the "Adversary," "There isn't anyone like him."

The scene shifts to God holding court with the various courtiers ("divine beings," "angels") gathered, including the "Adversary" (or the "Designated Accuser," or "the Satan"). This is not the Satan figure we find later in the Bible, but a courtier who has the role of saying, "Yes, but," or challenging God. Medieval courts had jokers who did this, though, as tempting as it is, I suppose it's not a clean comparison. Still we can read both courtroom scenes (see also Job 2:1–6) as banter between God and the Adversary. God brags on Job, "Have you noticed Job? There's nobody like him, full of integrity. . . ." The Adversary replies, "Yes, but he's not good for nothing, you know." Even in the awful challenge of these two scenes, we may still find witty telling.

The Adversary brings calamity on Job, on his wealth and his family. But the suddenness and scale of the four disasters, and the pile-up of each one's breathless, only-survivor messengers continue the outsized storytelling. The train wreck of messengers both heightens the catastrophe and prompts a smile. As one messenger is stammering out, "I alone escaped to tell you," the next one rushes in, blurting out even worse news.

Even Job's response to all of this might invite both amazement and a smile. He dramatically expresses his grief, then falls face down to worship, no complaints. It doesn't quite pass our "Is-that-normal?" humor test. In the story Job demonstrates his best-in-the-cosmos character, but then, what an odd, unusual character!

I invite you to try seeing humor in the dark, scene-setting story that opens Job. It will be easier when we get to Job's trash-talking friends. But as the book begins, I wonder whether you might see some grins in the gloom, perhaps even some that I've missed.

Women of Valor

The title itself piqued my curiosity: *A Year of Biblical Womanhood: How a Liberated Woman Found Herself Sitting on Her Roof, Covering Her Head, and Calling Her Husband "Master."* And I had enjoyed reading Rachel Held Evans' blog before. So when the Kindle store ran a special on the book, I snatched it. And read it. And liked it.

I wanted first to see how Evans used humor to carry on a serious conversation. Fans of her book bragged on her being disarming, thoughtful and witty, smart and funny, and on her showing "humor, humility, and truth." I agree. She uses humor to expose "public tomfoolery" for what it is, prompting laughter to shed light on the absurd, the contrived, and the exaggerated. She also creates space with humor to explore difficult subjects. I found many places where Evans makes readers laugh out loud while she's telling the truth.

I have not personally aspired to "biblical womanhood," but a burgeoning supply of books, audios, and videos promises to help those who do. Of course, they disagree on what it means and have a hard time choosing which biblical woman should be the standard. Should it be sneaky Rebekah, or Jael, who nailed a guy's head to the ground, or Huldah the prophet, or the women who traveled with Jesus, or the women who prophesied, taught, and were "elders" in the emerging church? A lot of the books focus on the hard-to-find woman of Proverbs 31, sometimes shortened (embarrassingly) to "P31 girl."

Evans, with the help of a Jewish friend and mentor, treats the Proverbs 31 woman beautifully as *eshet chayil*, a "woman of valor," a woman of courage, grace, and wisdom. She rightly describes how the song of Proverbs 31 honors women without turning them into stay-at-home moms who run home businesses and knit socks. But I'll let you read her for these insights.

As an Old Testament teacher, I've been puzzled by the rules-based views some hold of Proverbs 31. Let me tell you why. Lady Wisdom (or Wisdom Woman) stars in Proverbs: she helped God create the world, she calls out to everyone as teacher in the public square, she warns young men about themselves and dangerous Dame Folly, she puts on a huge banquet for all who will come and learn her wisdom, and much more. In later Jewish wisdom books, ones that many Christians include in their Bibles (in the "Apocrypha"), her prominent role grows ever greater. In the light of this, many interpreters see Proverbs 31 as a distillation of who Lady Wisdom is and what she teaches. Even as it uses the metaphor of a "woman of valor," it continues to teach both men and women how to live well. It models lessons of Proverbs about hard work, compassion, planning, paying steady attention to what needs to be done, and more. Men, too, are to be women of valor, even if they hesitate to pursue biblical womanhood.

Thanks to Rachel Held Evans for showing so well how humor can help tell the truth. Thanks, too, for her thoughtful study and interpretation in a time of loud and mixed voices. Her book will serve women and men well, I'm sure. It's very worth getting, even if it's not on sale.

The Hilarity of Grace

It doesn't happen only to people who win the one-in-a-million sweepstakes or who finally discover the perfect deodorant. Probably you, too, can remember when something wonderful happened to you, something so out of the blue and too good to be true that you didn't know whether to laugh or cry. If you're like lots of folks, you probably did both at once. Full of surprise and extravagance, grace can crash in like that, stirring up holy hilarity.

A song and a story from the Bible show hilarity at work. Psalm 126, the song, describes how, after a long exile, the Israelites got to return home. This was so unreal, so amazing, so improbable, they sang, that it seemed like a dream. But, they continued, their mouths "were filled with laughter" and their lips with song and exuberant shout.

The story is about the man, crippled for years, who was healed by Peter and John (Acts 3). After he stood, walked, and began to jump, he ran through the crowds in the temple precincts, leaping and shouting praise to God. The temple staff couldn't figure out how to handle such displays of visible, exhilarating joy.

In song texts like "there's a wideness in God's mercy like the wideness of the sea," people of faith witness to the extravagance of God's love. We wonder that God embraces us in love and accepts us in spite of all our defiance, klutziness, and failures. We see in Jesus that God will do anything to say, "I love you."

Such extravagance, such unbounded and surprising love, should fill our mouths with laughter, pour praise and songs out of our lips. It should stir up holy hilarity. Yet often it doesn't. Eugene Peterson observes that as a pastor his "most difficult assignment" is to help people develop a sense of "the soul-transforming implications of grace" in a culture that is in "persistent denial of grace" (*Practicing Resurrection*, 96).

Some folks, I'm sure, see themselves as self-sufficient, as self-made, as not needing grace at all. But more folks, I suspect, resist grace, perhaps because of its extravagance. "No, that's too much; I can't let you do this." "No, I don't deserve this; I don't want to be beholden to you."

Still others may receive grace as a burden of duty. They work to become worthy of it or to earn it. Or they may try to scale down its extravagance to make it an acceptable bargain. In doing so, they miss the wonder that grace is not about settling accounts or paying of penalties. God's grace is about pursuing with love, about wooing the beloved.

How much better if, instead of resisting grace or whittling it down to size, we were to receive it with joy and to share the lavish, undeserved love that God has shown us. Let's join in the gala of grace, with all the hoopla and hullabaloo and hilarity it can bring. Enjoy it, celebrate it, and share the extravagance of grace with one another and with the world.

Hubbub and Incarnation

Surrounded by the hubbub of Christmas, one friend worried that all this busy noise would overshadow the importance of Easter and the resurrection. "Christmas doesn't have much to do with anything," he grumbled, "except the incarnation . . . if you stretch it a little."

I want to assume he giggled a little as he grumbled. After all, the incarnation, the Eternal Word becoming human, is a *big* deal, even if we don't know exactly how to talk about it. Early on in seminary, Alan Richardson's book *Creeds in the Making* taught me that there are lots of ways to get it wrong, and that Christians in the early centuries of the church discovered most of them. Whatever confused thoughts we have now are usually just re-runs, though they can still stir up mischief.

Some folks focus mostly on Easter and even at Christmas sing that Jesus came to die. But the incarnation also means that Jesus came to live, to move into the neighborhood, to show us what God is like, and to show us what being human is like. We struggle to find ways to say that Jesus entered fully into our human condition and was the most extraordinary human we've ever known.

Many portray Jesus mostly as a man of sorrows, one who entered into and shared our grief. As Cal Samra points out, most Christian art historically, and even now, shows Jesus as sad, burdened, morose, or, at best, with flat affect. So it's hard for many to picture Jesus also as a man of joy, a person whose deep love and healing power takes root in joy and embodies the announcement of "good news of great joy."

The film *Matthew*, featuring Bruce Marchiano as Jesus, captures this joy better than most movies about Jesus that I know. Having read Sherwood Wirt's stirring book *Jesus, Man of Joy*, Marchiano describes what he discovered in reading the Bible to prepare for his acting:

> [It] became so blatantly obvious I couldn't believe I'd never caught it before. Suddenly it was everywhere, screaming from the pages of Scripture: joy!
>
> Jesus began jumping off the page at me as well—His realness and strength, the sparkle in His eyes, the spring in His gait, the heartiness in His laugh, the genuineness of His touch; His passion, playfulness, excitement, and vitality: His *JOY!*
>
> "Yes, Jesus smiled; yes, Jesus laughed. Jesus smiled bigger and laughed heartier than any human being who's ever walked the planet. It's been revelation to a lot of people both in and out of the church, their eyes opening wide after lifetimes of misunderstanding the Lord to be an aloof, pious, and sanctimonious figure.
>
> (Marchiano's, *In the Footsteps of Jesus*, 77)

Most of the Amazon reviews of the movie are positive, though some felt that it lacked *gravitas*, that Jesus smiled and laughed too much, and that this certainly would not be faithful to the Bible, even though the movie uses only the NIV text. Some reviews sounded like this: "The actor didn't seem at all like Jesus as portrayed in the Bible. Instead of Jesus as the Alpha and Omega, the Good Shepherd, the Lord of Lords, Emmanuel, the Messiah, the King of Kings, etc., it was like this portrayal of Jesus was designed to bring him down to our human level."

Without stretching it even a little, the point of the incarnation is that Jesus *did* live fully down at our human level. It is at once the most ordinary and most extraordinary human life we can imagine. Jesus' life among us was the most fully authentic human we've ever seen, full of love, integrity, joy, grace, and truth. It shows us that Jesus has shared our common life, and it shows what it possible for human life. It gives us reason, in the midst of Christmas hubbub, loudly and often to belt out "Joy to the world, the Lord is come" and to "repeat the sounding joy."

Stand-Up Jesus

While studying humor in the Bible, one author surprised me by saying that Jesus did stand-up comedy. Even in all the years of singing the gospel song "Stand up, stand up for Jesus," that had never occurred to me. But a lot of our great stand-up comics are Jewish, so I've been wondering what it would be like to imagine Jesus doing a Seinfeld routine on the hills of Galilee.

"Hey, it's good to see you all today! I hear there are some folk here from Capernaum. [pause, cheers] Yeah, nice town, even with Pete's mother-in-law. [rim shot] Anybody here from Nazareth? [pause] Guess not. Now *that* was a tough crowd! They nearly shoved me off a cliff. [laughter]

"How about a hand for my buddies, the Pharisees? [applause, maybe a jeer] They just got here from their prayers. [In stained-glass voice]: 'I thank you, Lord, that I'm not like those other guys.' [laughter] They've been giving me some great straight lines.

"You know, I kind of hate talking about other crowds, but that one the other day over on the next hill just didn't get it. I was joking with them about how they shouldn't let anything get in the way of the kingdom—you know, cut off your hand, lop off your foot, and all. And then this guy who'd been staring way too hard at Mary nearly tore his eye out. Hey, just listen and laugh and do the right thing. We already have plenty of blind folks to help."

Now I don't think Jesus did stand-up comedy, quite. But he did tell funny stories and create comic word pictures. He exaggerated, bantered, teased, and cajoled. His parables show off all kinds of improbable characters (or maybe the way-too-probable people we already know)—the crooked judge and nagging widow

(Luke 18:1–8), the neighbor leaning on the doorbell in the middle of the night and the sleepy crank who bails him out anyway (Luke 11:5–8), or the dishonest manager trying to bail himself out (Luke 16:1–9). Predating elephant jokes, Jesus told camel jokes—trying to thread a camel through the eye of a needle or, in trying to eat kosher, straining out a gnat while choking down a camel. (I'll bet that would have worked, too, with trying to get a speck out of the other guy's eye while you have a camel in your own.) And when the Pharisees and Sadducees tried to trap him with "gotcha" games, Jesus' easy wins surely amazed and amused the crowds.

A friend reminded me recently of the ditty, "Quaker meeting has begun. No more laughing, no more fun." In view of such (even self-inflicted) slurs on our reputation, it pleases me that one of the earliest modern books that called attention to Jesus' playfulness is Friend Elton Trueblood's *The Humor of Christ*. Elton argues, rightly, that we can't understand Jesus' teaching adequately when we fail to see his humor. Indeed, in some places getting the joke is the only way to catch on; it is the only way to take Jesus' message seriously. Humor teaches powerfully. It's a shame when we're so straight-laced that we don't get it.

Seeing Jesus' humor also can help us get to know Jesus better as genuinely joyful, warm, and friendly, as someone you would enjoy hanging out with. That makes a big difference for people who know Jesus mostly through word and visual images that depict Jesus only as sad, sorrowful, and scolding. Best of all, getting to know the joyful Jesus can draw us all more fully into the joy that Jesus is so eager to give us.

"Hey, did I tell you the one about the guy that got beat up on the way to Jericho . . . ?"

[This essay first appeared in Quaker Life *magazine and is used here with permission.]*

Imagine Them Smiling

What if humor were the only way to understand the Bible? Often seeing humor improves our understanding, but in some cases, humor offers the only way to make sense of the text. Elton Trueblood, in *The Humor of Christ*, argues that the story of Jesus' dialogue with the Canaanite woman gives a prime example.

The story (found in Matthew 15:21–28 and Mark 7:24–30) describes an encounter between a non-Jewish woman and Jesus, when he traveled outside of Israel to get some relief from the crowds. She was desperate to get healing for her demon-possessed daughter; Jesus was trying to hide. She found Jesus, threw herself at his feet, and begged for Jesus to act. He responded, "The children have to be fed first. It isn't right to take the children's bread and toss it to the dogs." She answered, "Lord, even the dogs under the table eat the children's crumbs." To which Jesus replied, "Good answer! Go on home. The demon has already left your daughter" (Mark 7, mostly from the *Common English Bible*).

Jesus does act compassionately, but the dialogue is disturbing. Trueblood says that any alternative to seeing humor in this account is "intolerable." Jesus appears here to be "rude . . . harsh . . . contemptuous." "Above all," he writes, "it is at complete variance with the general picture which we receive from the rest of the Gospel, particularly in connection with the poor and needy" (*The Humor of Christ*, 122). For folks who want to see Jesus as angry or mean, or needing to understand his message as well as we do, this is a gold mine. However, if we can recognize the cleverness and boldness of her bantering with Jesus, we can see the story in harmony with all we know of his loving presence and action, including his sense of humor.

Over coffee with Chloe, this story came up. She said she had just been talking about this with a friend who was puzzled by it. Trying to help, she told him, "Imagine them smiling." (By the way, Chloe gave permission for me to use her name and said she would be glad to receive donations.) "Imagine them smiling." Brilliant, I thought. The text doesn't give us facial expressions or vocal inflections; we bring those to it. Imagining Jesus smiling and even being a bit coy rather than being cranky makes a lot of sense, particularly when we remember Jesus' response in so many other stories.

My colleague Ron also tells me that this passage is very important to missiologists. They see this as one of the ways Jesus was teaching the disciples the wide range of the gospel. The sneaky gentleness of humor, as they watched, could well have had an enduring, powerful effect.

Since Chloe gave me this wonderful phrase, I have experimented with Jesus smiling in other stories. Though not always, often we smile with each other when we meet and talk. One occasion that intrigues me is the story of Jesus talking with another non-Jewish woman, the Samaritan woman at Jacob's well (John 4:4–42). I find reading with some sense of banter gives new life to the story. Perhaps while reading other stories about Jesus, you too can experiment with the phrase, "imagine them smiling."

Funnier than John

I'm sure that all of the Gospels use humor, including the bad-mouthed Gospel of John, but to me, Luke has the best sense of humor. New Testament scholar Joseph A. Grassi's book, *God Makes Me Laugh: A New Approach to Luke*, pushes me even more in that direction.

Though we can see lots of humor in Jesus' stories full of comic characters and twists in plot, Grassi shows the many examples of comic structures like surprise, reversals, the unlikely, upside-down, and backwards, features, which, as Frederick Buechner suggests, make the gospel itself comedy. In Grassi's words, we see in Luke "an upside-down' theology of surprise, grace, and shock" (*God Makes Me Laugh*, 28).

Grassi's opening chapter talks about "Divine and Human Laughter—The Roots of Comic Eschatology." (This was baffling enough that a proofreader changed "comic" in the title to "cosmic.") Grassi begins: "When people plan, trusting only in human power, God laughs; when God plans, working through human weakness, people laugh. In this paradox is found the roots of comic eschatology" (14). The whole Bible includes many examples, but the examples in Luke overflow.

Luke starts with an old woman and a virgin having babies, and recalls the words to Sarah, another old woman soon to be pregnant, "nothing's impossible with God." He then draws a sharp contrast between the stern baptizer John and the "playful and joyful" Jesus who feasted with unlikely (=forbidden) people, much to the dismay of pious folks. Jesus commented on the difference: "John the Baptist has come eating no bread and drinking no wine;

and you say, 'He has a demon.' The Son of Man has come eating and drinking; and you say, 'Behold a glutton and a drunkard, a friend of tax collectors and sinners'" (Luke 7:31–35). Try the interpretive principle "Imagine Jesus smiling" here, and think of folks you've heard get great laughs by pointing out such huge contradictions.

In a chapter called "Miracles and Comic Reversals," Grassi showcases the humorous paradoxes of the included becoming the excluded while the excluded are suddenly included, of the unclean becoming clean and the clean becoming unclean. Against the background of Sabbath and purity laws, Jesus heals on the Sabbath, touches lepers, and acts undefiled by contact with a woman haunted by years of continuous blood flow. He tells stories about bountiful banquets offered to the marginal and invisible folk, "the poor and maimed and blind and lame," outcasts who can never pay you back, a "feast of fools," in Grassi's words.

Other chapters speak of "crazy discipleship," "paradoxical parables," "humor in prayer," "foolish forgiveness," and the notable role of women in Jesus' mission, a huge reversal of common practice.

Luke is generally regarded as the author of both the Gospel of Luke and the book of Acts, and Grassi rightly explores how the themes and stories in the two books complement each other. They both capture the shock and surprise, the comic explosion of the kingdom of God. Luke, sometimes a traveling companion of Paul, witnessed the joy of all of this for himself, heard the early Christians tell him what they had seen, and freely shares it with his readers.

The good news is upside-down, exciting, and funny. Read Luke (and Acts) with eyes wide open, prepared to laugh and smile. [Grassi's fine book is a good read, too, and now available again at Wipf and Stock.]

Try Head First

You swallow a gnat before you know it, but how would you start to choke down a camel? I think I'd start at the big, hairy, spitting, biting end and work on down the long neck, humps, and gangly legs. My research confirmed this. Consider this recent headline: "Furious Camel Bites American to Death in Mexico over Can of Coca-Cola." A response to the article also put me on alert: "I hate camels. I believe they will kill you for sport." So leave your Coke behind and tackle the dangerous end first.

Better yet, just use your imagination. Straining out gnats is hard enough; ask any happy motorcyclist with bugs on her teeth. But picture a Pharisee trying to gobble up a whole camel. Does he hold him up over his head and gradually stuff him down his throat? Or does he leave him on the ground and drag him in bit by bit? Does he use any sauce or lube? According to Jesus, this didn't faze the Pharisees at all. What bugged them was the dang gnats.

Jesus' point was to ding the Pharisees a bit, but also to remind the rest of us to pay attention to the big stuff. He accused them of forgetting "the more important matters of the Law: justice, peace, and faith" (CEB). My point is that Jesus delivered a quick-hit, killer comic line and that, if we actually paid attention to it, we'd laugh out loud and maybe feel its sting.

Picture it. Enter in. Pay attention. Let it roll around in your head and heart. (See Matthew 23:23–24.)

Easter Laughter

April Fool's Day this year fell on the Monday after Easter. Perfect! I laughed to think that, on April Fool's Monday, Orthodox Christians in Greece and elsewhere were gathering to tell jokes and enjoy God's great victory in Jesus with humor. My colleague Tim Tsohantaridis reminds me that in Greece, at least, they celebrate every day of the week after Easter. In the same spirit, this past Sunday many American congregations observed "Holy Humor Sunday." *The Joyful Noiseletter,* edited by Cal Samra, reports each year the creative variety of ways that Christians have found to use humor to delight in the story of Easter.

One early way of explaining how Jesus' death and resurrection set things right uses a funny picture, one that uses trickery. Basically, God baits a great hook with Jesus and when Satan goes for the bait, God reels him in. (Not elegant, exactly, but the current favorite atonement theory isn't either.) Also using humor, a modern song by Carmen, "Sunday's on the Way," depicts Satan after Jesus' burial as panicky, worried that Jesus won't stay in the tomb. So Satan keeps phoning Grave to make sure Jesus is still dead. Carmen's audiences howl with joy and laughter when, on the third day, Grave desperately reports, "No! OH NO! OH NO ... SOMEBODY'S MESSING WITH THE STONE!"

In preparing for Easter, I read the four Gospel accounts of the disciples' experience that day. Their responses at first are what we might expect—surprised, stunned, dismayed, confused, heads swimming, full of wonder. But things change as seeing Jesus alive sinks in. For example, the King James Version of John 20:20 reports, "And when he had so said, he shewed unto them his hands and his side. Then were the disciples glad, when they saw the Lord." Glad. That's pretty tame. "Hi, I'm glad to see you." Contrast the reading in Peterson's *The Message*: "the disciples, seeing the Master with their own eyes, were *exuberant*." Peterson's reading is spot on. The Greek verb that is used here is a word for exultant rejoicing, for loud, festive joy. And this same word is used in two of the other Gospels. Again Peterson, "They returned to Jerusalem *bursting with joy*" (Luke 24:52). Similarly, in Matthew 28:8: "The women, deep in wonder and *full of joy*, lost no time in leaving the tomb. They ran to tell the disciples." Exuberant. Bursting with joy. Loud and festive.

Sometimes, when you get news that is too good to be true, you laugh and you cry, maybe staring in stunned silence or muttering, "No, this can't be happening." All at once. Jesus' disciples on that first Easter day heard and saw the best too-good-to-be-true news ever. It puzzled them and dazzled them. They couldn't believe it. But by the end of the day, I'll bet they laughed out loud while tears ran down their cheeks.

Smiling Persuasion

After seeing my brief note suggesting that the apostle Paul used humor when he wrote to Philemon, a friend emailed me: "I have not been able to read Philemon with a straight face for years! I was afraid I was being sacrilegious. I saw Paul as being a bit melodramatic and manipulative. I hadn't considered that Philemon may have been in on the humor!"

I'm sure that Philemon was in on it. While Paul was at Colossae, they had become good friends. They had worked and prayed, laughed and bantered together before. So when Philemon read (or heard) the letter, he could see the smile on Paul's face and the twinkle in his eye.

It's funny, but not frivolous. Paul writes to ask Philemon to risk taking revolutionary action, an action deeply personal, pointedly counter-cultural, and not simply theoretical. Paul pleads with Philemon to take his runaway slave back as a Christian brother. He's asking him to be a prime example of what he had written to Philemon's Christian community: "In this new life, it doesn't matter if you are a Jew or a gentile, circumcised or uncircumcised, barbaric, uncivilized, slave, or free. Christ is all that matters, and he lives in all of us" (Colossians 3:11 NLT). As friends often do, Paul uses humor to smooth the way.

Paul starts with lavish praise, highlighting especially Philemon as a model of love who cheers the hearts of his fellow Christians and brings delight to Paul. No doubt it's true and Paul is warm and sincere. But it's also too much, too lavish. A lot of us, I'd guess, smile and chuckle when we get exaggerated praise from a friend. We may also see caution lights and think, "So where is this going? What does he want?"

Just as the lights begin to flash, the letter turns. "Because you are so loving, I want to ask you to do something. I could insist, but I won't." (I paraphrase here and there.) J. B. Phillips' paraphrase continues here and catches the tone: "No, I am appealing to that love of yours, a simple personal appeal from Paul the old man, in prison for Jesus Christ's sake. I am appealing for my child. Yes, I have become a father though I have been under lock and key, and the child's name is—Onesimus!" How he piles on! Loving friend, help this old man, in prison for Jesus, and a new father, no less.

"Onesimus" is startling and fun. That Paul sent the we'll-never-see-him-again runaway to deliver the letter is mischievous in itself. In the letter Paul uses word-play to great effect: "My son 'Useful' [= 'Onesimus'] has been useless to you, but very useful to me, as if you were here yourself. But I couldn't do this in secret, behind your back, so I'm sending him (part of me actually) back to you, knowing that he'll be very useful to you." Then, still with a smile, dynamite: "Please treat him like a Christian brother, not a slave. . . . Welcome him as you would welcome me."

So what do you think? Is Philemon now sucking air, smiling, saying, "so *this* is where that was going!"?

Paul doesn't put down the humor hammer yet. Still in jail, Paul says, "If he owes you anything, put it on my tab. I'm good for it. I won't even mention that you owe me your life." To close, I imagine with a huge grin, Paul taps into his lavish beginning, "Of course, your love is so amazing that I know you'll do even more than I ask." And, by the way, "I hope to visit you soon. Get ready." No pressure.

The setting of the letter also makes me smile. It's not really a private letter. All the folks who admire Philemon as a model of Christian love will hear it. Probably with Onesimus sitting right there.

Paul works Philemon, no doubt. But he does it as a dear friend, full of love and high regard. In that context, he uses humor to wade into deep waters and to give Philemon the insight and courage he needs to do the hard, but right, thing. I'm glad for friends who have done the same for me.

Select Bibliography

Adams, Douglas. *The Prostitute in the Family Tree: Discovering Humor and Irony in the Bible*. Louisville, KY: Westminster John Knox, 1997.

Arbuckle, Gerald A. *Laughing with God: Humor, Culture, and Transformation*. Collegeville, MN: Liturgical, 2008.

Buechner, Frederick. *Beyond Words*. San Francisco: HarperSanFrancisco, 2004.

———. *Telling the Truth: The Gospel as Tragedy, Comedy, and Fairy Tale*. New York: Harper and Row, 1977.

Duke, Paul D. *Irony in the Fourth Gospel*. Atlanta: John Knox, 1985.

Grassi, Joseph A. *God Makes Me Laugh: A New Approach to Luke*. 1986. Reprint. Eugene, OR: Wipf & Stock, 2009.

Hyers, Conrad. *And God Created Laughter: The Bible as Divine Comedy*. Atlanta: John Knox, 1987.

Jemielity, Thomas. *Satire and the Hebrew Prophets*. Louisville, KY: Westminster/John Knox, 1992.

Kilpatrick, Joel. *GOD, That's Funny: Getting God's Sense of Humor*. Westlake Village, CA: LarkNews, 2012.

Palmer, Earl F. *The Humor of Jesus: Sources of Laughter in the Bible*. Vancouver, BC: Regent College Publishing, 2001.

Peters, David A. *The Many Faces of Biblical Humor*. Lanham, MD: Hamilton, 2007.

Phipps, William E. *The Wisdom and Wit of Rabbi Jesus*. Louisville, KY: Westminster/John Knox, 1993.

Radday, Yehuda T. and Athalya Brenner, eds. *On Humour and the Comic in the Hebrew Bible*. Sheffield, UK: Almond, 1990.

Shutter, Marion Daniel. *Wit and Humor of the Bible: A Literary Study*. Boston: Arena, 1893. (Available through BiblioBazaar, LLC.)

Trueblood, D. Elton. *The Humor of Christ*. New York: Harper and Row, 1964.

Walker, Steven C. *Illuminating Humor of the Bible*. Eugene, OR: Cascade, 2013.

Whedbee, J. William. *The Bible and the Comic Vision*. New York: Cambridge University Press, 1998.